# HAVE YOU SEEN THESE CHILDREN?

# HAVE YOU SEEN THESE CHILDREN?

*a memoir*

VERONICA SLAUGHTER

SHE WRITES PRESS

Published 2020
Printed in the United States of America
ISBN: 978-1-63152-725-8 pbk
ISBN: 978-1-63152-726-5 ebk
Library of Congress Control Number: 2020904537

For information, address:
She Writes Press
1569 Solano Ave #546
Berkeley, CA 94707

She Writes Press is a division of SparkPoint Studio, LLC.

Interior design by Tabitha Lahr



Names and identifying characteristics have been changed to protect the privacy of certain individuals.

# AUTHOR'S NOTE

In 1959, four young children—Valorie, Veronica, Vance, and Vincent—went on a journey that changed their lives forever.

They were innocent bystanders caught between two worlds: one filled with love, stability, and happiness; one marked by instability, separation, and deception. Why was this happening, and how were they going to endure? Instinctively, they knew the answer was to stick together, no matter what or where the next day brought them. So this band of inseparable warriors used the ties of love, the power of prayer, and the will to survive—their only weapons—to get through each day.

With one misguided decision by their mother, these four children went from living a perfect life to living in circumstances that left them confused and frightened. All in the same day, they experienced unconditional love and a total disregard of their well-being.

I was one of those children. The majority of this book is told in the voice of my eight-year-old self as I tumbled down the rabbit hole of my new reality. When our lives were turned upside down, I immediately knew that my number one job was to protect my three-year-old brother. The bond we forged during this time would last a lifetime.

*"There is no greater agony than bearing an untold story inside you."*

—Maya Angelou

# INTRODUCTION

My memories of my childhood are a collection of short movies that play over and over in my head. I've kept most of them locked away my whole life, fearing what might come to light if I watched them.

Now, though, I'm finally ready to face the past. Putting these memories on paper has revealed why I am who I am and unveiled parts of my life I had refused to acknowledge until now. Two memories from this period are crystal clear: the day my father took me and my three siblings from our mother, and the day we were found. We were like books that were checked out of a warm and safe library, only to be returned four forever-years later. We were turned back in somewhat worn, a little abused, and with a few missing pages. We had traveled through many hands, some caring and some not so much. During those four years, I prayed every day to find my way home—in one piece, if possible.

In 1959, the year my father abducted us, I was eight, my sister, Valorie, was nine, and my two brothers, Vance and

Vincent, were seven and three. We could not have known what awaited us; we had no idea we'd live in six states and attend seven schools before our journey came to an end. Those were uncertain times; we never knew what the next day would hold. The one thing I knew for sure was that we had to stick together. Our survival depended on it.

Writing about our journey hasn't been painful in the way I thought it might be; instead, I've experienced unexpected joy as I've discovered myself and the true meaning of love. Writing this story has given me a perspective I'd never before considered. I can now say that I understand myself and my siblings for the first time. Putting our life on paper has been one aha moment after another. What I feared for so long has been transformed into an awakening.

A psychologist once told me, "If a child is beloved the first three years of their life, they are capable of enduring challenges throughout their life." I'm here to tell you how true this is. The unconditional love my mother gave me in my early years kept me strong when I needed it most while my father held my siblings and me captive.

Most of my life, I've wondered why I've done the things I've done, why I've never felt I'm enough, why I've held other people's feelings to be more important than my own. In my heart, I always knew I'd find the answers in my childhood. Looking into my past was like digging for treasure; I had to be willing to get dirty to find what was buried there.

I hope my story will help you see that facing your fears from a place of love can heal many wounds. You may discover a strength you didn't know existed, and what you find may be more valuable than you could have imagined. We don't have to be slaves to our past. Writing is what set me free. Find what will set you free, too—and wherever your self-discovery leads you, never give up on love and kindness, especially toward yourself.

---

This book is dedicated to my beloved siblings, all of whom are gone too soon; I feel a responsibility to tell my story, our story. There weren't any four children closer than the Slaughter kids. We protected, loved, and lived for each other. We talked about growing old together and sharing the life we dreamed of with each other. We were going to make it, make it together. Our story was never supposed to end this way.

This book is also for my son, Francis. I love him the way I've always wanted to be loved.

Unconditionally.

And now, the story of four young warriors and their lost years.

## Chapter 1:

# THE AMERICAN AND THE ARISTOCRAT

It was 1946. WWII had just ended and the man who would become my father, Robert (Bob) Slaughter, was twenty-four and fresh out of the army. Bob had been stationed in the Philippines for several months, and he'd grown to love Filipino culture and food, and especially Filipina women. Life was sweet, so Bob decided to make Cebu, Philippines, his home.

According to my father, he first laid eyes on my mother in the summer of 1947. He was riding on a Jeepney, a converted US Army Jeep repurposed for public transportation. Thousands of these Jeeps were left behind after the war. The Jeepney drivers competed against each other by painting their Jeeps in bright colors and decorating them with shiny ornaments and fringes, all to attract riders onto their makeshift bus. The two adornments they all had in common were a picture of the Blessed Virgin Mary, which they stuck to their windshields, and a Sacred Heart of Jesus, which they hung from their rearview mirrors.

It was a hot and humid afternoon, and everyone was covering his or her mouth with a handkerchief to keep from breathing in the dust the Jeepneys kicked up. The Jeepney Bob was in was packed and all he could think about was getting off at the next stop. As the Jeepney slowed down, however, he saw two women waiting to board: a beautiful young woman and her maid, who held an umbrella over her and carried her packages. Bob took one look at this vision of beauty and sat back down.

Several men stood up, waiting to see whose seat the young woman would choose. For their chivalry, they received a demure smile and a "*Salamat*," or thank you.

As the story goes, my mother crossed her legs and that was all it took for my father to fall in love. He vowed at that moment that he'd marry this beautiful woman.

Unbeknownst to Bob, Elisa (Lily) Ortiz-Orat was a sophisticated, well-educated, and untouchable woman with beauty, brains, and breeding. His chances were slim to none. For one thing, no one was allowed near Lily without going through Soling first. Wherever Lily went, Soling accompanied her. Soling was thin and dark and wore her straight black hair in a tight ponytail that swung back and forth as she kept pace with Lily. Soling had been Lily's personal maid since she was a child and took her job very seriously.

Three stops later, the young woman and her maid stepped off the Jeepney with Bob right behind them, close enough to ask her name. Of course, when he did, Lily ignored him.

Soling, finding the American inappropriate, yelled, "*Pahawa!*"—"go away" in Cebuano.

At this, Bob dropped back—but not for long. He was handsome, charming, and persistent. He continued to walk alongside the attractive, evasive woman, making sure to keep an umbrella's distance from her bodyguard. He remained polite but refused to be swished away by a maid.

Lily Orat, 1942

"I teach at the University of San Carlos," he announced boastfully.

Lily focused straight ahead, expressionless. Soling started walking faster, glancing back every few seconds to make sure the American wasn't getting too close while being sure to keep the umbrella reached out to cover Lily's head. The Philippines is a brutally hot country and the sun's rays are intense, so one of Soling's many jobs was to keep the blazing sun off of Lily's creamy skin. Lily wasn't a typical Filipina; she was fairer and taller, with big, beautiful eyes.

Soling made sure to keep distance between the American and the Aristocrat. As they approached a bakery, Lily slowed down and then abruptly turned and entered the door with Soling in tow.

Bob decided not to follow, even though the smell of *pan de sal* was enticing. He knew if he pursued her too hard, it might backfire. Unlike in America, where women spoke freely with men they didn't know, in the Philippines women from prominent families required a formal introduction.

---

For days, Bob hung out where the Jeepney had stopped that fateful afternoon, hoping to see the beautiful young woman again. When he finally spotted Lily, Soling spotted him too and immediately stood sentry between them, making sure the bold American wouldn't get past her.

This time, Bob managed to follow them long enough to learn that the object of his desire lived in a two-story house at the end of Jones Avenue. The large wooden house was decorated with white crocheted curtains and orchids in every window. The yard around the house was well manicured and smelled of the Sampaguita flower. It belonged to a man named Segundo Orat.

Whoever Segundo Orat was, Bob thought, he must be important.

Bob was not used to being ignored by anyone, man or woman. He was the talk of the town, standing out wherever he went with his Scotch-Irish good looks. At six foot two, with sandy blond hair and green eyes, he screamed *Americano* in the Philippines, causing a stir everywhere he went. Women wanted to be near him, and men wanted to know him. General MacArthur's words, "I shall return" still rang in most Filipino's ears; they loved Americans.

During his first few months in Cebu, Bob had made a myriad of influential friends at the popular nightclubs he frequented. Many Filipinos looked up to the Americans amongst them—literally and figuratively—and it wasn't what you knew but *whom* you knew that counted in the Philippines. Bob had quickly realized that being popular was expensive and required an impressive job that paid well. So, being well connected, he'd convinced the university that he held advanced degrees in agriculture—not bad, considering he had all of an eighth-grade education—and talked his way into a job at the University of San Carlos. Apparently, his word as an American was good enough for Mr. Martinez, the headmaster of San Carlos.

Not long after he started, Bob developed a program for incubating chicken eggs and even built a large incubator that held hundreds of fertile eggs himself. The administration was impressed. Having lived on a farm in Colorado paid off. The program was so successful that the university added agriculture to their curriculum. Bob was more popular than ever and was right where he wanted to be. The college girls were beautiful, and the pay was acceptable, but most important, it was the impressive job he was looking for. He could now flaunt not only his good looks but also his position.

And now he'd found a woman worth the effort.

Armed with a prestigious job, Bob focused on meeting Lily. "No" was not an answer he would accept, so he came up with an idea: he asked Mr. Martinez if he knew Segundo Orat, the man who lived in the big house on Jones Avenue. If anyone knew this prominent man, he figured, Mr. Martinez would.

Luckily for Bob, Mr. Martinez and Mr. Orat were old friends. That's when Bob found out that Segundo was the superintendent of schools. Bob quickly launched a plan to meet with Mr. Orat regarding the incubation project, and Mr. Martinez agreed to arrange a meeting. Bob then described the beautiful young woman he saw on Jones Avenue. He asked who she was, and whether she was related to Mr. Orat.

Mr. Martinez looked at Bob suspiciously. Meeting Mr. Orat was one thing, he said, but meeting his daughter, Lily, was out of the question.

Now Bob knew the young woman's name and status. He assured Mr. Martinez that his interest was only in Mr. Orat.

Mr. Martinez suggested that Bob bring a gift to the meeting—he said doing so might help get funds to expand the project. Segundo loved good cigars and fine cognac, so off to the black-market Bob went—and, being an American, he managed to procure a box of Cuban cigars and a bottle of Courvoisier.

Segundo Orat was a respected educator in Cebu, a vigorous negotiator who was not easily fooled. He demanded honesty and hard work from the people around him, especially his thirteen children. In return, he was fair and generous.

Segundo was married to Felicisima Ortiz, a Spanish aristocrat. The thousands of hectares the family owned—a sugar cane plantation called Hacienda Mandoma—came from the Ortiz side of the family.

Coming from such a family, Lily wouldn't be allowed to go out with just anyone, much less an American. She was her parents' favorite. Both indulged her every whim. She loved clothes, especially the light gray silk stockings that were all the rage, and even during the war, Lily managed to get what she wanted, sometimes by refusing to eat. (With her nineteen-inch waist, everyone in the house was concerned about her slimness.)

Bob no longer waited for Lily where she got off the Jeepney. He knew she would notice his abrupt absence, and she did. This was all part of Bob's elaborate plan. When the day came for Bob's meeting with Segundo, he dressed professionally and brought detailed information on the incubator project. They met at San Carlos, along with Mr. Martinez, and discussed the need to feed families as well as provide skills training. The incubator project delivered both.

Bob and Segundo got along better than expected. They shared many of the same interests; both, for example, were voracious readers with insatiable appetites for world news. When their meeting was over, Bob received his funding and Segundo the gift of cognac and Cuban cigars. Segundo was so delighted, he invited Bob to dine with him at his home the following week.

You can imagine how clever Bob thought he was. Yes, he liked Segundo, but meeting Lily was his goal.

---

The night Bob came to dinner, the whole Orat house was buzzing. It was a big deal to have a dinner guest, much less an American. All the maids were on their toes. Every Filipino delicacy, from *lumpia* to *pancit*, was being prepared. You could smell the pork *adobo*, *biko*, and *ensaimada*. The long, ebony dining table was covered with a lace tablecloth, on top of which were perfectly placed embroidered linen napkins, Felicisima's prized bone china, and crystal glasses from Spain. If everything wasn't just right, you'd hear about it from the mistress of the house; she was fastidious about her *balay*, her home. Even the maids were dressed in their best clothes.

Bob arrived right on time, with a heavy wooden crate filled with bottles of Coca Cola on his shoulder. Coca Cola was like liquid gold in the Philippines. I'm sure everyone was curious about where he'd procured this treasure.

Bob and Segundo talked shop in the *sala*, the great room, which was filled with hand-woven rattan furniture, beautiful mother-of-pearl lamps, and small *Molave* tables that were smooth to the touch. The walls were decorated with religious paintings and hanging orchids.

Finally, Felicisima announced dinner was ready. She had a regal look about her, carried herself tall and proud. Her beautiful, long black hair was held up with a carved ivory comb, and she wore a traditional Filipina Maria Clara dress—a billowy, loose-sleeved blouse made of pineapple fibers worn over a colorful, ankle-length skirt. You knew Felicisima was in charge just by looking at her. Bob saw instantly where Lily had gotten her good looks.

Segundo was pure Filipino: short, stout, and wickedly smart. With his insatiable desire to learn, he spent his free time writing and reading books, magazines, and newspapers. He believed that knowledge was power and with this power, there wasn't anything a person couldn't accomplish.

Everyone started toward the dining room. Segundo's three sons came to the table first and stood patiently behind their chairs out of respect for their parents. Felicisima walked in with Bob, and Segundo followed close behind. No one ever sat until their mother did.

Before the war, Lily had six brothers. Three had been killed fighting with the Americans against the Japanese, leaving Jess (Jesus), Cesar, and Nap (Napoleon) to fill the shoes of their sacrificed brothers.

Felicisima sat, then everyone else took their seat. Segundo led a prayer, giving thanks for the food, their guest, and prosperity for the Philippines, before everyone began eating.

There was plenty of small talk. Felicisima explained the different foods on the table and encouraged Bob to try them all. He was the perfect guest. Not only did he eat everything on his plate, he also requested seconds. The boys wanted to know about popular American movies and music. They talked about Hollywood and roads paved with gold. There were lots of laughs and Bob fit right in. Then Bob asked Felicisima if she had only boys. She smiled and told him they had seven daughters. Bob knew better than to ask where the girls were.

After an incredible dinner, Bob and Segundo retired to the veranda, where they smoked cigars and drank cognac. The light breeze was pleasant and kept the mosquitoes away. It started to get late, so the seven daughters and three sons lined up one by one to say good night to their father. Each did *la mano*, which is placing the back of an elder's hand lightly to your forehead as a sign of respect. Lily was the last. She did *la mano* to her father's hand then kissed him on his cheek. She turned her head slightly and smiled at Bob.

For Bob, carrying that heavy crate of Coca-Cola up twenty stairs was worth that one small smile.

My life had been set in motion.

Chapter 2:

# BLINDSIDED

Bob worked his way into Lily's family, starting with her brothers. He soon became close friends with Jess, Cesar, and Nap. All it took was his black-market alcohol and American cigarettes. In no time, the Orat brothers considered Bob one of their *barcada*, their group. They fished and frequented bars together. Bob was one of them.

Eventually, Bob was formally introduced to each of the sisters: Antonina, the eldest, Presentacion, Maria, Sofia, Elisa (Lily), Mercedes, and, lastly, Priscilla. The brothers had no idea Bob had his eye on Lily, but Soling knew better. She knew what Bob was up to and watched closely for any impropriety. She wanted something to report to the mistress of the house, but Bob was clever and never crossed the line.

As time passed, Bob was invited to many more Sunday dinners at the Orat *balay*. He brought Cuban cigars for Segundo and beautiful flowers for Felicisima. (Felicisima loved flowers and grew a variety of colorful orchids that were planted all along the front of Jones Avenue.) Before long, Bob was also taking the Orat clan out for *merienda*, a midday snack. These socials were filled with jokes and mischief and focused on the younger members of the family.

In time, Bob was able to take long walks with Lily, albeit always with Soling close behind. He had cunningly woven his way into Lily's life.

Segundo was blindsided.

After several months of outings, there were fewer chaperones, but Bob was never alone with Lily. He was, however, able to talk to her for hours and got to know everything about her and her family.

Soling disdained the boldness of the American. She could see Lily was taken with Bob.

Bob's ability to converse easily with everyone impressed Lily. He was boisterous but polite, talkative but listened intently. Bob was even taking lessons in Visayan, Lily's dialect. They practiced their new languages on each other, which always resulted in laughter.

Then something mysterious happened: Bob disappeared without a word. No one saw the popular American for more than a week. Many people were worried, especially Lily. She had grown used to Bob's visits. She enjoyed his stories and his company was entertaining for the whole family. Everyone knew Lily liked Bob, but also knew their relationship was only a friendship. Her parents would object to any involvement beyond that.

One morning, after Bob had been missing for several more days, a messenger came to the Big House. He handed a note to Lily that read, "Come to Cebu Hospital, quickly." It wasn't signed but Lily knew it had something to do with her friend Bob. She grabbed Soling and went straight to the hospital.

---

Bob was in a private room, which was rare in any hospital. There was a young nurse standing by; a mosquito net covered the bed with an IV pole on the opposite side. Bob's eyes were closed, and he looked pale, his face scruffy and thin. Lily sat on a chair next to him and reached under the mosquito net to touch his hand. A doctor came in and whispered to Lily that Bob was gravely ill. He had contracted cholera and was not expected to live. (Many people died of cholera in the Philippines in those days; it was often contracted just by drinking the water.)

As Lily gently stroked Bob's hand, he turned to her slowly and opened his eyes. Tears ran down Lily's cheeks. Soling waited outside the doorway of the room, her face showing no emotion.

Bob was trying to speak, but Lily couldn't make out his words. The doctor lifted the mosquito net and advised her to move in closer. Bob spoke with labored breath, "Lily, if I live, will you marry me?"

Shocked, she looked up at the doctor and shook her head from side to side. The nurse in the room wept softly.

The doctor told Lily that Bob was delirious, and she should promise him anything to bring a dying man comfort.

Bob kept asking over and over.

Finally, reluctantly, Lily said, "Yes." The doctor and nurse witnessed the sad scene.

Soling wasn't buying it. "*Ayaw!*"—"Don't!"—she said, and then, "*Adto na ta!*"—"Let's go."

Bob started coughing and the nurse moved quickly toward the bed. Lily got up and stepped aside to give the nurse room to do her job. The IV pole on the opposite side of the bed was not connected, which Lily thought was odd; with cholera, fluids were administered constantly. But she figured the staff knew what they were doing.

The doctor told Lily that Bob needed rest and encouraged her to come back in the morning. She begged to stay and wanted to send Soling to get her brothers and inform her father. She wanted to get word to the headmaster at San Carlos to bring their family priest as well. But the doctor advised against any more visitors, and said it was Bob's wish to tell no one except her. The nurse chimed in that the hospital had already arranged for the American's last rites, the Catholic sacrament for the sick and dying. A local priest was already on his way.

Lily cried all the way home. She couldn't believe the exuberant young American was dying. Soling continued to show no sympathy. Lily felt uneasy about giving her word to marry Bob but felt it was the least she could do for a dying friend. Being a devout Roman Catholic, she lived by the Ten Commandments, of which "Thou shall not bear false witness" is the ninth. Segundo had taught all his children the importance of a person's word. From Bob's many long conversations with Lily, he knew this.

---

Lily went to mass that evening and again the following morning. She prayed for Bob's eternal soul. She told her family Bob was dying and the doctor had strict orders not to have any visitors with the exception of Lily, at Bob's request. She asked her brothers to get in touch with Bob's mother in Colorado. Would his mother want him shipped home?

Segundo knew most of the doctors at Cebu Hospital and was prepared to help in any way. He asked Lily the doctor's name. She told her father she'd been so upset she'd forgotten to ask but would get more information as soon as she went back the next morning. Even though Segundo wanted to help, he respected Bob's wishes by holding off visiting or using his influence with Cebu hospital.

Lily and Soling hurried back to the hospital the following morning. When they arrived, Lily wiped her tears before quietly entering Bob's room. To her astonishment, he was sitting up in bed, laughing and talking with a different young nurse. His color was back, and he had shaved. His curly blond hair was washed and combed, and the room smelled like perfume.

Bob wore a big smile on his face as he turned toward Lily.

Confused, Lily managed a nervous smile in return and asked Bob how he was feeling.

"It's a miracle, Lily," he said, "I woke up feeling like a new man."

Lily excused herself and ran out of the room. She moved quickly through the halls of the hospital, looking for Bob's doctor. Because she didn't know his name, she described him to anyone who would listen. Bob's private room was reserved for people of means, however, and many times these patients had private doctors. No one Lily asked seemed to know what doctor she was talking about.

Lily raced back to the room. Bob was now dressed and sitting on the edge of his bed, and the young nurse was listening to his chest. She seemed to be standing closer to him than necessary. When the nurse was done, Bob turned and held his hand out toward Lily, "This is my future *asawa*"—"wife"—he said to the nurse.

Soling looked on from the doorway with horror. Lily was frozen.

The nurse put her hand over her open mouth. Lily couldn't speak either; a thousand thoughts ran through her head.

*What am I going to do?*
*I gave my word.*
*How am I going to tell my father?*
*Do I love this man?*
*What have I gotten myself into?*
*Oh, Saint Jude, help me.*

⸻

No one ever knew if Bob had really had cholera, as his doctor was never seen again. Bob would later claim he'd been too sick to remember anything. Lily believed that Bob's recovery was a miracle. She convinced herself that marrying him was God's will—and she kept her promise. An honorable person never goes back on their word once it is given. Lily had to make the choice of going against her father or going against God. God won.

Lily knew her father would never support a marriage to an American. He was the only one she feared, and rightfully so. Not only was she marrying outside the culture, she was going against her father and bringing shame on the family.

Segundo was furious when he heard. He vowed never to speak Lily's name again. Felicisima tried to reason with her husband, reminding him Bob had a good job and was well respected. Segundo wouldn't listen. This was the one and only time Lily had ever gone against her father's wishes, and now she no longer existed to him.

Segundo refused to attend the wedding and forbade Felicisima from attending as well. Felicisima cried in private, knowing better than to argue the point with her husband. Once Segundo's mind was made up, the discussion was closed. Thankfully, all Lily's siblings did attend the wedding, as did her closest friends. Her brothers supported her decision. They liked Bob and secretly felt their father was being old-fashioned, though they never would have said that to his face.

Even though Felicisima wasn't allowed to attend her daughter's wedding, she wasn't going to let Lily get married in just any dress, so she had the best seamstress in Cebu make Lily's wedding gown. When the dress was done, Soling carried the box with its precious cargo to Lily's sister Sophie's house. Soling didn't say a word to Lily regarding the marriage, it wasn't her place. Her job now was to be by Lily's side.

Included in the bridal box was a long, flowing veil made of Spanish tulle and a silk pouch holding Felicisima's favorite pearl earrings, a gift from her mother; now they were a gift to her favorite daughter. Like Lily, they were simple but elegant.

Of course, it was a Catholic wedding. Bob invited all of his friends. He arranged a lunch at a popular restaurant and a honeymoon to Baguio, a mountain retreat away from the dust and heat of the city and a destination of the wealthy. It was pleasantly cool, and the scenery was spectacular.

Lily's youngest brother, Jesus, walked her down the aisle. She was stunning in her long, white, virginal gown. The tulle veil covered her anxious face; her jet-black hair flowed around her face. Lily was a vision of beauty as she moved toward her *paman hunon*, future husband. Her long limbs and nineteen-inch waist were well defined in the fitted silk gown. Lily and Jess continued the long walk toward the altar as Bob stood next to the priest, eagerly waiting for her.

Happy Wedding Day

The Santo Nino Basilica was built in the 1730s by the Spaniards. The church walls were heavily laden with statues of saints; the relic of Santo Nino de Cebu was the most precious item inside. Lily was lightheaded from the strong smells of hundreds of burning candles and incense throughout the church. She held tight to her brother's arm as they moved closer to the inevitable. As Jess released his sister to her soon-to-be husband, Lily glanced to her left, where the statue of St. Jude stood, and she said a silent prayer, asking for strength.

Bob looked Hollywood handsome. He didn't wear the traditional wedding *Barong Tagalog* but a white tuxedo instead. No one in town had ever seen anything like it, except in the movies.

Inside the bridal veil, Lily's eyes began to fill with tears—tears of sadness, not joy. Her beloved mother and father were not there to smile at her. She wanted their blessings. She wanted her father's hugs and her mother's kisses.

This was supposed to be the happiest day of her life.

## Chapter 3:

# SHATTERED

Valorie Elisa was born nine months after Bob and Lily married. They lived in a small house not far from Jones Avenue. Soling had her hands full with the cooking, cleaning, and marketing. Of course, Bob was never around. He continued to enjoy his popularity, and his eye for the ladies hadn't waned. Soling wasn't surprised, and Lily pretended not to notice; being a mother was her greatest joy.

Bob quit his teaching job at San Carlos. He told Lily he was busy making deals and had no time for the university. He wanted a business that would bring in more money, not more chicken eggs. Bob tried to convince Lily that he was doing it for her and their growing family, but Lily felt she had everything they needed. Her father was all that was missing in her life. He was what she prayed for most.

When Valorie was four months old, Lily instructed Soling to bring the baby to Jones Avenue, the Big House.

She wanted her father to see Valorie Elisa. For over a year, Segundo had not spoken Lily's name or answered her letters. No one was allowed to mention anything about her in his presence. Segundo held steadfast to his word, but Felicisima was not going to be kept from her daughter and new granddaughter; she visited frequently.

It was a bright Sunday morning when church bells rang all over town to mark the end of Mass. Sunday was a busy day for the many churches in Cebu. Soling knew the family patriarch would be in his study after Mass; no business was ever conducted on the Lord's day. She walked carefully up the twenty steps leading to the large wooden doors of the Big House, opened the doors slowly, slipped off her wooden *bakia*, and walked silently toward the study, carrying the beloved bundle.

She froze in the doorway as Segundo looked up disapprovingly; but then, shaking off her fear, she stepped forward and said, "*Apo nga babaye*"—"Your granddaughter." Before Segundo could say a word, Soling held Valorie out to him.

Under any other circumstance, he would have scolded Soling for disturbing him. In this moment, however, he hesitantly but gently took Valorie Elisa from Soling's caring arms. He held the baby's warm body against his, then tenderly peeled back the delicate blanket. He took one look at the beautiful sleeping baby and fell in love.

"What's her name?" he asked without looking away from her tiny face.

"Valorie Elisa," Soling said.

Valorie had jet-black hair, like her mother, and creamy white skin. Her eyelashes were so long and curly they didn't seem real. She was a *mestiza*—part Filipino, part American. All was forgiven the second Segundo laid eyes on her.

Nothing could have made Felicisima happier. Segundo, too, was elated to have his daughter back in his life, and now a beautiful granddaughter as well. It was like nothing had ever happened between Lily and her father.

⸻•⸻

One day, Soling informed her mistress that Lily was pregnant with a second child. Segundo immediately sent over another maid to help with meals and washing clothes. Lily had never cooked or washed anything in her life. She was their *paboritong anak nga babaye*, their favorite child. Now, however, she worked on her cooking and sewing skills for her new daughter and future children. Motherhood suited her perfectly.

Bob began drinking more and was home less. He made friends with a group of Americans looking to start businesses. Labor was cheap, and the American dollar was coveted. Late one night, he came home to tell Lily that they were the proud new owners of a seaplane. According to Bob, he had won the plane in a poker game from one of his American friends.

Bob was known to tell tall tales, so Lily didn't know if she should believe him or not.

"This plane is the answer to all our prayers," he told her. But Bob didn't pray, and Lily would never pray for a plane, so that didn't fly (pun intended).

He named the seaplane the Lone Ranger and it became the lucrative new business he was looking for. He flew merchandise from island to island, dropping off and picking up packages all day, every day. The more than seven thousand islands that make up the Philippines are close together, which made island hopping easy. His new business instantly turned a profit.

One night, Bob brought home several gold bars the size of sticks of butter. By then, Lily had learned not to ask questions. She never knew where or from whom those bars came, and they disappeared as fast as they had appeared.

The black market was big business in Cebu, and rumors started going around that Bob was transporting contraband. Out of respect for Segundo, no one mentioned that his American son-in-law was suspected of smuggling. It was easy to pay off officials in the Philippines if you were an American; the almighty dollar was king.

Suspicious-looking individuals begun casting eyes on the Lone Ranger, however, and Segundo himself started asking questions as well. When he heard the rumors, he questioned Bob. Of course, Bob convinced Segundo that the rumors were being spread by people who were jealous of his success and wanted to put him out of business. Bob's stories were always elaborate, so full of detail that anyone listening couldn't imagine he'd be lying. Bob could have sold a dead man life insurance.

Lily and Bob moved to the island of Samar a few months before their second baby was due—supposedly because of his business. The truth was, Bob didn't want to be under Segundo's watchful eye. He no longer had to impress Segundo Orat. As father of Segundo's beloved grandchild and husband of his favorite daughter, he was untouchable.

On Samar, they lived in a town called Calbayog. Being the good wife, Lily went along with what her husband wanted to do. She hated leaving her family in Cebu and felt alone without them. She knew Bob would be gone more than ever, so she kept busy with Valorie and preparing for the arrival of her new baby.

As Lily got closer to her due date, everyone tried to reach Bob, with no luck. By the time she went into labor, she was more than a week overdue and Bob was still nowhere to be found—an especially upsetting situation because there wasn't a hospital close by, and the plane could have made the difference between life and death for Lily and their unborn baby.

When Lily went into labor, Soling hurried to get the town's midwife; most women in the Philippines had home births. When the midwife arrived, she immediately recognized that this was going to be a difficult delivery.

Lily's friends streamed in, bringing food and maids. As the maids busied themselves laying out food, candles were lit and rosaries prayed—offerings to God for Lily and her baby's safe arrival.

As labor progressed, everyone worried that Lily might die; she was tiny, and the baby was abnormally large. A priest was called after the first twenty-four hours of labor in case one or both didn't make it.

Finally, after forty-eight hours of great effort on the part of mother and midwife, I was born. An exhausted Lily asked for her baby as Soling gently wiped the sweat from her face and arms with a cool cloth. At first, the midwife thought I was stillborn; then I let out a loud cry, signaling that the frightening ordeal was over. A collective sigh of relief was heard throughout the household, followed by jubilant cheering. (According to the midwife, it was a miracle we both survived, because not only was I large but it was also a dry birth.) The priest made the sign of the cross over Lily and her new baby, then blessed the house and everyone in it. Mom and I had made it. We were warrior women.

It was October 28, 1951, the Feast Day of St. Jude, patron saint of lost causes. The saint that my mother prayed to daily had brought me safely into the world on his celebrated day. I weighed in at eleven pounds, the size of a six-month-old by Filipino standards. I had blond hair and blue eyes and was the first white baby most people from the town had ever seen.

Everyone talked about how I'd fought to live. They claimed it was because I was a *Waray*. The *Waray-Waray* were a fierce people in Samar's history, the most notorious warriors in all of the Philippines—a people who feared nothing and were feared by all. I was born a warrior to a warrior; it was in my blood.

Veronica Theresa was the name Mom gave me. I was named after Saint Veronica, who wiped the face of Jesus before he was crucified. She was compassionate, devoted, and brave. When Soling announced my arrival, my godmother had the local church ring their bells every hour on the hour for the next two days; forty-eight hours of bells for the forty-eight hours Mom and I had fought for our survival.

The small town of Calbayog had never witnessed anything like me before. A line formed around our house; people wanted a glimpse of the miracle baby.

The moment Soling laid eyes on me, she loved me more than life itself. That day, Soling was designated my personal maid. I was her only job, just like Lily had been her only job when she was born. Soling held me up in a colorful blanket for all to see.

The people of the town looked on in amazement at my whiteness and size. Soling later told me that I was the most beautiful baby anyone had ever seen. Presents were lovingly placed in front of our house: Baskets filled with papayas, bananas, mangos, and green coconuts. Sweet-smelling leis of *Sampaquita* flowers and even a *lechon baboy*, a roasted baby pig. It was time to rejoice. Spontaneous celebrations broke out all over town.

*Lolo*, which was what my sister and I would soon call our Filipino grandfather, made sure we had everything we needed. We were his greatest pleasure and could not have been loved more. He loathed Bob by this point but tolerated him for our sake. Lily told her father not to worry; she was happy being a mother and raising her girls.

Shortly after I was born, Lily convinced Bob to move back to Cebu. She needed her parents and help with the children. My grandparents were thrilled. Felicisima—or *Lola*, as we called her—oversaw everything, often scolding Soling for carrying me constantly. Lola told Soling I'd never learn to crawl, much less walk, if she didn't put me down. Valorie and I were pampered and surrounded by our extended family and their love.

Just when things couldn't have been better in Cebu, Bob had an announcement to make. One evening at Sunday dinner, when the whole family was gathered at my grandparents' house, he stood up, a complacent look on his face, and enthusiastically announced, "I'm taking my wife and daughters to the United States."

There was dead silence. In 1953, taking us to America was like going to another planet.

Nothing could have prepared us for what was to unfold.

I was almost two years old, and our perfect life was about to be shattered.

## Chapter 4:

# TWO WORLDS

After Bob's shocking news, my grandparents sat in stunned silence. Everyone at the table stared at Bob, then at Lolo. From the kitchen's entrance, Soling made the sign of the cross over herself.

"When?" Lola asked. "Why?"

"In two weeks," Bob said. "Because I want my children raised in the United States, where there is more opportunity."

Lola stood up from the table and pleaded with him to delay the move. "Please, wait till the girls are a little older." Begging was beneath my lola, but the fear of losing us was overwhelming.

Bob's mind was made up. Lola picked up Valorie and held her tight.

You could have heard a pin drop, until Lolo finally spoke. He swallowed his pride and offered Bob a piece of the family plantation and an administrative position at San Carlos, a position that paid well. Like my grandmother, Lolo would give Bob anything if it kept him from taking us to America.

Lola tried to reason with Bob, reminding him that the family wouldn't have maids or drivers in America. There wouldn't be *lavanderas* to wash our clothes or *cocineras* to cook our food. Who would clean the house and watch the children? I'm sure my grandmother worried for her daughter. She'd heard how hard life was in America with no maids.

Bob's final answer to all the pleading was, "Lily is my wife and the girls are my children. No one is going tell me what to do regarding my family."

Lily was as shocked as everyone else. Bob had told her he'd sold the Lone Ranger because of mechanical problems. Was that just another tall tale? She wondered if the angry strangers coming to our house looking for him had anything to do with his decision to leave the Philippines.

Before this declaration, Lily had no idea Bob was planning to take us to America; her head was spinning with the news. She said it was impossible to be ready on such short notice and suggested that Bob send for us once he secured a job, but he wasn't having any of it. Nothing anyone said could change his mind. Valorie and I were American citizens, and he was taking us to the US, with or without his Filipino wife. And there was no way Lily would let Bob leave with her precious daughters; where we went, she went. So, there was only one option: she would go along with Bob's plan.

Lily wondered what our life would be like in America. Bob reassured her that it would be easier. We wouldn't need maids, he said, and he talked about washers and dryers to clean our clothes, machines to wash our dishes, irons that plugged into the wall instead of using hot coals, vacuums for cleaning floors, TV dinners that rendered cooking unnecessary. Lily had no reference for any of these things. Bob told her life would be easy, and we'd be happy. He also promised to bring us back to Cebu every year to visit.

Lily stopped trying to reason with her husband once she realized she wasn't going to win. She would just have to be stronger than ever; she offered a silent prayer to St. Jude.

---

At the airport on the day of our departure, there was disbelief and tears. Bob pried me out of Soling's arms, and my mother took Valorie from Lola. Lolo had already said his good-byes to his daughter and granddaughters at the Big House. He would not give Bob the satisfaction of seeing his grief.

We didn't have time to say good-bye to all of our relatives. Many of them lived on other islands. Soling wanted to come with us, but Bob said no; he was determined to cut us off from the only world we knew. He was taking us to a new world—his world.

---

When we arrived in the United States, everything was different. Bob fought with Mom all the time, and America was nothing like he'd promised. There were no friends or Sunday family dinners. Mom constantly cleaned, cooked, and cared for us. When Bob finally found a job as a car salesman, we moved from Denver to Boulder, Colorado.

In 1953, Vance Edward was born. Even when Mom was exhausted from caring for three young children, she made time to have fun with her *mga anak*, her babies. Unfortunately, Bob was not only drinking now but also hitting Mom. She no longer had her family to protect her. She cried privately but put on a happy face for us.

I was four years old the first time I remember my father yelling at my mother. He was so loud and angry; I couldn't figure out what I'd done wrong. I was sure it had something to do with me, since I was the only one in the kitchen with them. My father threw his coffee cup at my mother and when it broke on the yellow linoleum floor, a piece flew up and cut my mother's leg; it started to bleed. I ran to her, crying that I was sorry, and held her leg tight. She picked me up and comforted me, telling me it was alright.

From that moment on, I was afraid of my father.

Even with all Mom's duties at home, she still found time to study, and in 1955 she received her master's degree in English from the University of Colorado, Boulder. Elisa Orat Slaughter graduated with honors, fighting ignorance and prejudice every step of the way. Students and faculty looked down on her for the way she looked and the way she spoke. One teacher said he didn't want her in his class because he couldn't understand her English; he told her to come back when she could "speak correctly." Mom's answer to him was, "Fine. I don't understand you, either."

My mother had a BA in English from the University of the Philippines, and her grammar was perfect; it was her skin color the professor objected to. World War II was still fresh in many minds, and some couldn't tell the difference between Filipinos and the Japanese. Once, when we were in a supermarket, someone called my mother a "dirty Jap." That was pure ignorance, but when her advisor asked if it was true that Filipinos had tails, that was unabashed racism. Other faculty members also tried to make her quit, not knowing my mother didn't quit; she was a warrior, strong and proud.

She taught us to be honest, first and foremost, and to always hold our heads up in the face of adversity.

After Mom received her master's degree, we moved to Los Angeles, where Bob got his dream job with the Sheriff's Department. He felt important, and it didn't hurt that the uniform attracted women. Many nights, he came home drunk, but Mom never questioned him; his anger was worse than whatever the answer might be.

---

On December 17, 1956, Vincent Robert was born. With four children under the age of six and an abusive, alcoholic husband, my mother gave up her dream of pursuing a doctorate. When Vincent was six months old, Bob was fired from the Sheriff's Department after being spotted in Chinatown drunk and in uniform. He quit looking for jobs after that.

With Bob not working, Mom started teaching at St. Theresa's Catholic School. Valorie and I were lucky, because we were able to attend school there. Vance and Vincent were too young, so they stayed with a neighbor during the day; Bob couldn't be trusted to watch them.

At the end of each day, Mom cooked, gave us baths, and prayed with us. She taught me how to pray the rosary and instilled in all of us the power of prayer. "God will hear you if you're patient," she told us. We all got hugs and kisses before falling asleep. Bedtime was my favorite time of the day.

One Sunday morning, Mom made our favorite breakfast: waffles. Waffles were for special occasions, so we were all excited. Bob was in a good mood and sat at the table with us. As we ate, Mom asked him if we could go back to the Philippines for a visit. It had been almost four years, and she wanted her family to meet Vance and Vincent. She appealed to Bob's ego, reminding him how popular he was and how everyone there looked up to him. He agreed to go.

Even though we knew nothing about the Philippines, Valorie, Vance, and I started clapping, because Mom looked happy; this was definitely a special occasion.

Mom wrote to my grandparents. She didn't mention the abuse; she only shared good news, including the fact that we were coming home. She told them to make space for her and her four children at the Big House. She didn't mention Bob. My grandparents were overjoyed when they received the news.

---

When we arrived in Cebu City, our uncles, aunties, and cousins were all there to greet us with tears of joy and lots of hugs and kisses. When Soling spotted me, she ran and picked me up. I was six years old now, and I didn't remember who she was, but I knew she loved me. I wrapped my arms around her neck and told her I loved her; I felt tears on her cheek when she pressed it against mine. My uncle Jess shook my father's hand and helped with the luggage.

When we got to Jones Avenue and walked up the twenty steps, Mom closed the door behind her and stood on the veranda—the same place where Segundo and Bob had drunk cognac and smoked cigars years before. There, standing with her brothers, Lily told Bob she wasn't going back to the United States. She was home and was not giving up the children; she wanted a divorce.

Bob was furious. He argued with Lily, saying she'd deceived him, and he wasn't going to let her get away with this; we were American citizens and his children.

For a while, Lolo sat quietly, smoking a cigar. Then he calmly told Bob that if he tried taking us, he would have him charged with kidnapping. Lolo was now a powerful politician; if necessary, he could make Bob's life very difficult.

Lily was careful in her explanation to her parents about why she was leaving Bob. She didn't mention the bloody lip or the black eye or the trip to the hospital for a *fall* when she was eight months pregnant with Vincent. (When I was five, my father had reached across the table and hit my mother, causing her to fall off her chair.) Lily didn't mention her shame from the constant verbal abuse. Instead, she claimed life was simply too hard in the United States.

Lolo knew better. He knew how strong his daughter was; Lily never gave up on anything. But he didn't question her. He was just happy to have his two new grandsons, his granddaughters, and his beloved Lily home where we belonged.

Once again, life was perfect. Parties at the Big House, picnics with the whole family at San Remigio Beach, and, best of all, Soling constantly fussing over me. Our life was full of laughter and kisses. Mom wore beautiful dresses and red lipstick and was happier than I had ever seen her.

I learned early: if you are patient, God answers prayers. He'd answered Mom's, after all.

No more tears, no more bruises, no more yelling, no more Bob.

## Chapter 5:

# LEE'S COFFEE SHOP

The four of us kids now lived with our mother in Cebu. I never asked where our father was; it didn't matter to me. We stayed with our Lolo and Lola in the Big House until Mom opened her very own business, Lee's Coffee Shop. There was an apartment above the coffee shop and that became our new home; Soling stayed with us too.

Mom named the coffee shop Lee's because that's what the people in America had called her. It was located on Osmena Boulevard. Lolo said President Osmena was the best president the Philippines had ever had. Many Americans lived nearby on Osmena Boulevard, and Mom said that's what made it a good location—Americans, not like Filipinos, had money to buy things.

When Mom opened the coffee shop, she told us we needed to be good helpers because Soling couldn't do everything. My grandparents were sad to see us leave, but Mom wanted to take care of us on her own. She was smart, and she could do anything she wanted to do—that's what Lolo said.

I was glad we still got to see our grandparents on Sundays. Lolo read poetry to Valorie and Lola taught me to dance the *ti-nik-ling*—a Filipino dance done between two long bamboo poles. The girls wore bright dresses and the boys white shirts with rolled up black pants. The bamboo poles were held on both ends by other dancers who kneeled on the ground and banged the bamboo together. You were supposed to jump in and out between them: *Clack, clack. Bang! Clack, clack. Bang!* If you weren't fast, you got your foot caught between the poles. It was lots of fun. You did this while dancing barefooted and twirling your arms above your head. I got my foot caught a lot and that made everyone laugh. Lola said it took years to learn how to do it well.

Living above Lee's Coffee Shop made it easy for us to help Mom, and we got to see her all the time. Our small apartment also had everything we needed. There were two small bedrooms and a large living room. All the rooms had huge windows with fancy bars on them that were pushed out far enough for us to sit with crossed legs in the windowsill. We'd sit and watch as people rushed by. Maids pulling small carts filled with fresh fruits and vegetables, children kicking a rubber ball that was almost flat, the fish lady carrying a big round basket on her head with fish that were still moving. You could see all kinds of things sitting in the window; it was exciting. Once I even saw a man kissing a lady on the lips.

We had a round wooden table in the middle of our living room with a pretty tablecloth made of plastic that our American grandmother had sent us. We ate at this table, played games on it, and did our homework on it too. Sometimes, Valorie and I would move it so we could sing and dance to the radio or make circles with our bodies in our hula hoops until we dropped to the floor. We had fun every day.

There were two beds in one of the bedrooms. Valorie slept with Vance and I slept with Vincent. I was supposed to share a bed with my sister, but Vincent wouldn't leave my side, so that's how it ended up, Vincent and me. I loved my little brother so much.

The first time I saw my baby brother, I was five. Immediately, I felt he was mine. We were still living in America when my parents brought him home from the hospital. I knew I had a brother before anyone told me he was a boy. When Mom put him down on the bed that first night, she asked me to keep an eye on him. I put my face next to his and whispered that I'd protect him and love him forever, because he was my baby. My face was so close to his face that I felt his eyelashes tickle my cheek. His little mouth kept pushing in and out. I loved Vincent more than I loved anything in the whole world.

Our beds were covered with bedspreads that my mother made. She let Valorie and me choose the colors. I chose big blue and green flowers, and Valorie chose red and yellow squares. Mine was the prettiest, but we could play checkers on Valorie's bedspread.

Soling slept on the floor between our two beds. The purple mat she slept on wasn't even soft, but she liked it. She always kept an eye on us, even when we were sleeping.

Soling didn't use a mosquito net. She said mosquitoes didn't like her—but boy did they love to bite Vincent. He moved so much at night that sometimes his leg or arm would end up outside our mosquito net. In the morning, his little arm or leg would be covered with itchy red bumps. Soling would rub them with alcohol and that made the itching stop. She always knew what to do, just like Mom.

Mom's room had a bigger bed. My auntie Sofie made Mom's bedspread—knitted it with two long, skinny needles. It took her a really long time. Mom had a dresser in her room with a big mirror on it. She had a statue of St. Jude and the Blessed Virgin Mary on one side and a fan that moved back and forth on the other. She also had face powder and red lipsticks lined up in front of the mirror. Her room always smelled good, like baby powder—clean and fresh. Sometimes I'd sneak into her room at night to snuggle. She never pushed me out.

Downstairs, Mom's coffee shop was packed, mostly with Americans. Mom had been right about it being a good location. It was the place to go for *real* brewed coffee—most places only served instant coffee called Sanka, and Americans liked Mom's coffee much better—and to meet friends. Mom also made her yummy donuts every day. My American grandma in Colorado had taught her how to make these special treats. They were soft and sprinkled with sugar, and you could only find them at Lee's Coffee shop.

Lee's Coffee Shop: Valorie, 9 and I, 8 in 1959
just before we were taken

The customers loved sitting at our counter, telling stories about the United States and what they missed most. I'd hide behind the counter on the floor and listen to them talk about movies and their president, Eisenhower. Soling always found me and called me "*Maldita*," for misbehaving and not finishing my chores.

At Lee's, Mom was more popular than a movie star. She was beautiful and smart and spoke English well. And because we'd lived in America, she was like one of them. Men were always asking her to go to dinner. Every time, she smiled and said, "No thank you, how about a cup of coffee instead?" and everybody laughed. I was never sure why people laughed when Mom said that.

⸻

It was a sunny Saturday morning at the coffee shop, and we were all downstairs, getting ready to open. Saturdays were our busiest days and there was a lot to do before our first customer. Each of us had a job. My main job was keeping an eye on Vincent, because he was only three. Mom said he was still a baby and needed to be looked after all the time. I kept a close watch on him, but I knew he wasn't a baby; he didn't wear diapers anymore.

Vincent and I were folding napkins when, suddenly, a man came bursting through the front door of our coffee shop making all the souvenirs hanging on the door rattle like chimes. He had a bunch of presents under one arm and a big bouquet of flowers under the other. It was Dad!

We were surprised. We hadn't seen him in over a year. He'd missed my first holy communion. Vincent clung to me like he was afraid; he didn't recognize our father. Dad had a big smile on his face when he yelled, "Where are my little Indians?"

None of us moved at first—not till Valorie went running toward him, screaming, "Daddy, Daddy!" Then Vance, Vincent, and I ran after her.

He looked so handsome with his suntan and dark sunglasses. He scooped us up, one by one. He smelled like soap and cologne all mixed up. He hugged and kissed us. He swung me in a big circle, holding me tight. At that moment, I loved my dad. Why couldn't he be like this all the time?

Dad was wearing a white shirt and a pair of white pants with no wrinkles. They looked like they were brand-new. It was hard to keep clothes ironed in the Philippines because it was so hot and humid; that was what made my white uniform blouse wrinkled at the end of the day, even though it was perfect when Soling put it on me in the morning.

I turned around and looked at Mom. Her mouth was open like she'd just seen a ghost. She wiped her hands on her apron and slowly came out from behind the counter. She stuck out her hand like she always did when she said hello to someone. Dad scared her when he lifted her up and kissed her. She pushed him away with a funny look on her face and said, "How are you?"

Dad told Mom he was a brand new man. I wondered what he meant. How had he become a *brand-new man?* I would have to ask Mom later.

Dad said he'd stopped drinking and had started a business. Mom raised her left eyebrow up high, like she did when she didn't believe something. Whenever I told Mom I was done with my chores or homework, she would lift her eyebrow the same way.

Dad handed Mom the bouquet of flowers and a white

envelope full of money. Next, he gave each one of us a present. We were so excited, we started screaming and clapping. We knew the presents were from America by the wrapping paper.

Mom asked Dad to have a seat at the counter, and she served him freshly brewed coffee and a hot donut.

He smiled. "These taste just like my mother's."

Finally, Mom smiled too.

While Dad and Mom talked about grown-up business, we carefully opened our presents. I helped Vincent so he wouldn't tear too much of the fancy paper. Soling stood by to pick up all the pieces, flattening and folding them neatly. She had never seen such shiny, thick paper. The Philippines didn't have this kind of wrapping paper, and Soling saved everything; nothing was ever wasted in the Philippines.

They were bathing suits! We'd never owned a bathing suit before. Filipinos wore shorts and T-shirts when swimming in the ocean. Lola said bathing suits were indecent and only tourists wore them, but our bathing suits were the most beautiful we'd ever seen. Mine was turquoise with silver fish, Valorie's was pink with white dots, and Vance and Vincent's had pictures of boats and surfboards on them.

"Did you bring a present for Soling?" I asked Dad.

"Of course!" he said and handed her a little package.

I wanted to see what was in it, but Soling refused to take it. She turned around and went back into the kitchen to make more donuts. The coffee shop was going to open soon, and there was still lots to do.

I looked over at Mom and Dad. They weren't yelling or fighting, and even looked like they liked each other a little bit. There was some smiling but mostly talking.

Soling kept looking out from the kitchen. She was upset, and I wished she would have opened her present; then, I thought, she would be happy too.

I saw Dad trying to grab Mom's hand. When he finally got her wrist, he said, "I have a favor to ask you, Lily."

---

My life was about to change forever.

## Chapter 6:

# THE HAPPIEST PLACE ON EARTH

Dad was still holding Mom's wrist when he said, "Please, Lily! Please come meet my American friends."

He told Mom he was doing business with them; they had "cattle money." I'd never heard of money called "cattle." I figured it must be something in America, because you didn't see many cows in the Philippines. Instead, there were water buffalos that helped the farmers plant rice.

Mom always looked after us, especially when it came to our dad. He would ask to take us shopping or to lunch but Mom always said, "Not today." She never let Dad take us anywhere when he came to visit, which was probably why we hadn't seen him that past year. I think she didn't trust him because he'd hurt her when we lived in America.

Today was different. Dad was different. He was nice to everyone, even Soling. Mom seemed to have forgiven him. I couldn't remember my dad ever having been so nice to her.

He said he'd turned over a "new leaf." Americans sure said lots of things that didn't make sense. What did leaves have to do with anything?

Whenever my father showed up, Soling stayed close by with a watchful eye. She said she had eyes on the back of her head, though I knew she was just kidding about that. She wore the same look around my dad as the one she had when she watched for shoplifters trying to take our souvenirs hanging on the coffee shop door, or when little children came around with their palms out, begging for money. Soling shooed them away because it wasn't good for business. I wanted to give them donut holes sprinkled with sugar, but Soling wouldn't let me. She said if I did, we'd have hundreds of dirty children at the door. I prayed for those little children every night when I said my rosary.

On this Saturday morning, Soling stood closer to me than usual. Dad's American friends were staying at a nearby hotel and wanted to meet all of us. They had a new business in the city and wanted Mom's advice. She was so smart, everyone asked her for advice. I would hear customers say, "What do you think I should do, Lee?" and Mom would give them ideas.

Dad's American friends had also invited us for lunch at the big, fancy hotel where they were staying. It even had a swimming pool. That must be why Dad had bought us bathing suits! He said we'd have a great time.

We started jumping up and down again, begging Mom to let us go. We were screaming so loud that she put her hands over her ears and finally said, "Okay, okay." I ran into the kitchen and told Soling that we were going swimming, but she'd have to wear a bathing suit because we were going to a real swimming pool, not the ocean.

Dad still had Mom's hand. He kissed it and said, "Thanks, Lily. I'll bring my friends by when I drop off the kids. We can all talk then."

I didn't know what that was all about, but I did know I hadn't ever swum in a real swimming pool, and I wanted to wear my new turquoise bathing suit with the silver fish.

We had a telephone in our coffee shop that the American customers paid us to use. Dad asked Mom if she wanted to call his friends.

"No, it's okay," she said. "You can take them, but they need to be back before noon."

Vance and I grabbed Mom's arms and started pulling her from behind the counter. We were spinning with joy.

Mom looked at us. "I'm not coming," she said. "You're going with your father."

I stopped jumping up and down. I didn't want to go without her.

"Soling and I have too much to do," she said, shrugging. People lined up before we were open; they could hardly wait to get their brewed coffee and warm donuts. And visiting with Dad had put Mom behind. She needed to prepare food, fry dozens more donuts, and get more coffee brewing. Soling had to stack the dishes, wipe the counter, sweep the floor, and finish folding the napkins Vincent and I had started. Mom never used paper napkins because it was wasteful, so Soling washed and ironed the cloth ones every night.

Mom thanked Dad for the envelope and told him twice to make sure we were back before noon. Dad wrote down the number of the hotel and the names of his friends on a piece of paper, then handed it to Mom. We hadn't finished our chores, but Mom said it was okay, we could do them when we got back.

Mom packed a large box of hot donuts for Dad's friends. She wrote something on the box, but I couldn't read her cursive. I loved to look at my mother's handwriting. It was like a beautiful drawing, with lots of loops and curls.

Soling kept saying, "*Mo kuyog ko nila*"—"I will go with them." I didn't want to go without Mom or Soling, but I also knew they had lots of work to do before opening the coffee shop. Mom told Soling not to worry—that we'd be back in a few hours and the hotel was only a block away.

Valorie, now nine years old, was the only one with a watch because she was the eldest. Mom told her it was her job to keep track of the time and to remind Dad not to be late. Then she packed our new bathing suits, small towels, and extra underwear in small plastic bags with handles, each one a different color. Mom always did that so we'd know which bag belonged to who.

At the last minute, Mom said maybe Vincent should stay because he was too young to be near a pool. But he started crying and ran to me; where I went, Vincent went.

"I'll be in the pool with them the whole time," Dad reassured her, and I told her I'd keep my eyes on Vincent every minute. I promised in the name of God, because that's what you say when you really mean something.

As I grabbed Vincent's hand, I got a sick feeling in my stomach. I thought maybe I'd eaten too many donut holes. Then it was hugs and kisses from Mom, then Soling, then Mom again. She instructed us to be polite and behave ourselves.

Soling was not smiling. She looked upset. She held my hand tight until we got to the car. As we started piling in, I remembered my rosary. I never went anywhere without my rosary. I felt safer with it, especially when Mom wasn't around. "Wait, Daddy, wait!" I cried, then jumped out and ran upstairs to get it.

When I came down, Mom said, "Don't lose it, you'll need it for Mass tomorrow."

"I won't!" I climbed into the backseat.

Dad took the box of donuts from Mom and told her how much he appreciated her letting us go, then kissed her cheek. It was the first time in three years she had let us go anywhere with him. I was happy she trusted him again. I waved to her and Soling out the back window. Mom waved back, the piece of paper Dad had given her with his friend's phone number on it gripped in her fingers. Soling didn't wave; she just stood there like a statue. I kept waving until they disappeared.

Happiest place on earth

I felt that sick feeling in my stomach again.

After driving for a while, Dad said, "Okay, now for the big surprise." He told us we were flying to America! We would have television and bicycles, and we would go to Disneyland, the Happiest Place on Earth!

There was more screaming and clapping in the car.

But not from me.

"What about Mom and Soling?" I asked.

He told us our mother knew all about the trip and had wanted it to be a surprise. He said they would be following shortly, but first they had to pack our things.

I felt confused. Why didn't Mom tell us? Why did Dad have to beg her to let us go if she knew about it? I didn't like this surprise. I asked about Lee's Coffee Shop. Dad said not to worry, that Mom had lots of people to take care of the coffee shop. I couldn't imagine who would make the brewed coffee and donuts. Only Mom and Soling knew how to do that. What about all our customers? What about our apartment upstairs? What about all the souvenirs hanging on the coffee shop door? Did Lolo and Lola know we were going to America?

The sick feeling in my stomach was worse now, and it wasn't going away.

Chapter 7:

# UP, UP, AND AWAY

We arrived at Lahug Airport carrying only our bathing suit bags. I got out of the car and felt lost. Valorie and Vance were still excited, but I wanted to cry. I pulled Vincent closer to me as we followed Dad into the airport. It was crowded, dusty, and dirty. The airport was open with a big tin roof over the top. I was scared but didn't want to show it. The more I looked around at all the strangers, the more worried I got. I asked Valorie what time it was.

I didn't remember ever having been there before, but it reminded me of the outside market where Soling went every day. She never let me go to the market with her because she was afraid I'd get dirty—or worse, lost.

I was carrying my and Vincent's bags. He wanted me to pick him up, but I didn't want to put our bags down. Mom told me never to do that because they would get stolen. Soling said there were pickpocket people in crowded places.

The pickpocket people could take your watch off your wrist or money from your pocket without you knowing. I pulled my rosary out of my pocket and put it around my neck, then tucked it under my T-shirt to make sure no one saw it. I kept my eye on Valorie's watch.

Vincent was hot and tired and started to fuss. I convinced Valorie and Vance to hold our bags so I could pick him up. They would have said yes to anything at that moment, because all they could talk or think about was Disneyland.

Vincent squeezed my neck, and I did my best not to drop him. He was so heavy.

"Where's Mommy?" he asked.

"I'll play Mommy until our real mommy comes," I told him.

There was no place to sit, so Dad told us to stand together near a big pole. "Don't move until I get back," he said, "or else."

Or else what? It had been a long time since I'd seen my dad, and I'd forgotten how different he was from Mom. He talked different and didn't watch over us like Mom and Soling did. I remembered how afraid of him I'd been when I was little. When he said, "or else," did that mean he was going to hit us like he'd hit Mom?

There were people rushing all around carrying boxes tied with rope, squawking chickens hanging upside down, and big suitcases. We didn't have suitcases, and I didn't think we had enough clothes for America.

I saw barefoot little boys and girls selling cigarettes and magazines on bamboo trays and other children wearing only dirty T-shirts, squatting on the ground and begging for money. I couldn't remember a time when I had been out of Soling's sight since coming back to Cebu, except when I was in school. She would never leave us by ourselves in a public place. Who was going to look after us now?

We were still standing next to the big pole and there was no more jumping up and down or clapping.

"Are we still going swimming?" Vance asked Valorie.

"Be quiet and wait until Dad gets back," she said.

I could tell Vance was tired too. He wanted to sit on the ground, but I told him it was too dirty and to lean against the pole instead. I wished we were back at the coffee shop, helping Mom and Soling. Vincent was hungry, and our bags got heavier every minute.

I carefully looked around, checking the lines for Mom and Soling. I saw Dad talking to some men. He looked upset and didn't seem nice anymore. I wanted to know what was going on but couldn't leave Vincent. I waved my arms, trying to get my father's attention, but he wouldn't look at me, even though I was sure he saw me. What was happening?

"What time is it?" I asked Valorie again.

She looked at her watch. "Almost noon."

Mom was going to be worried if we didn't call her right away.

A man in a uniform started talking to Dad. He wasn't a policeman but looked important. I waved my arms at Dad again. I wanted to tell him to please call Mom, but he was busy putting money into a white envelope like the one he'd given Mom. He handed the envelope to the uniformed man; the man put it in his pocket. The man kept looking over at us. What was Dad telling him? It was noon now; Mom and Soling were waiting! Did Mom really know we were here? My stomach was beginning to hurt bad, like the time I ate green mangos.

Dad and the uniformed man started walking toward us. When they got close, I reached out and grabbed Dad's arm. "We have to call Mom," I said.

He ignored me and jerked his arm away. The uniformed man asked our names. We answered, one by one.

"We're going to Disneyland!" Vance said excitedly.

The man didn't smile. "Follow me." He put his hand on Vance's head and pushed him forward. "Hurry," he instructed.

Everyone started walking fast, but I didn't want to go. When Vincent and I caught up with Dad, I begged him to wait a little longer. We couldn't leave without Mom.

"Okay," he said, "then go over there and wait by yourself." He pulled Vincent's hand out of mine.

I panicked. I couldn't stand in the airport by myself, and Vincent couldn't leave without me. Vincent reached his other hand toward me and started to cry. Mom had told me to take care of my brother, so I grabbed his hand.

"The plane is full, so your Mom and Soling are coming on the next plane," Dad said.

Now I started crying. I tried to hold it back but couldn't any longer. I didn't know what to do. But I didn't cry for long; I knew if I continued to cry, Vincent would cry too. So I dried my eyes with the hanky Soling always made me carry in my pocket.

I wanted to be home, doing my chores.

We walked up to a counter, and Dad handed the man behind it two little green books. The man opened both and looked down at us. He wrote something, smiled, handed the green books back to Dad, and said, "Have a safe flight."

*Was flying not safe*? I wanted my mother. We couldn't leave without kissing her good-bye.

There was a pretty lady at the counter in a blue jacket that said P-a-n A-m on it. She wore a small matching hat. Before starting for the plane, Dad gave her Mom's box of donuts. What was he doing? Why was he giving the box away to a stranger? I wanted to take them back. I wanted to see what Mom had written on top of the box; now I would never know. *Please, St. Jude*, I prayed, *find my mother*.

By the time we climbed the steps leading up to the plane, we were tired and hungry. Even Vance was quiet, which he never was. Valorie was the only one still excited. She was asking Dad all kinds of questions about America.

After we found our seats, Vincent started to cry again. I looked around and saw plenty of empty seats. *Why did Dad say the plane was full?*

Another pretty lady wearing the same blue uniform came up to us. She asked if we wanted Coca-Colas. That made everyone feel better. We didn't get to drink Coca-Cola with Mom unless it was a special occasion. She made us drink evaporated milk mixed with water. Soling put sugar in mine to make it taste better.

Dad called the lady a stewardess and said we could ask her for anything. The stewardess brought us all Cokes and *siopao*, rolls with meat inside them. Dad asked for rum to go with his Coke. When she came back with Dad's rum, she gave each of us an American candy bar called Baby Ruth. I wondered why they would name a candy bar after a baby; they didn't eat candy.

Vance and Valorie had their faces stuck to the window. As the plane started moving, I closed my eyes and held my rosary tight. We moved faster and faster, and then I felt the plane leave the ground. Suddenly, we were flying up, up and away—away from Mom, away from Soling, away from Lee's Coffee Shop. What was going to happen now? I looked at

Vincent, asleep on my lap, and wondered how long I was going to play Mommy.

Dad was talking to the stewardess and laughing. She looked *mestiza* like us, tall with light skin and eyes. Dad held her hand and asked for more rum, then winked at her. Mom said winking was flirting. Americans winked at Mom at the coffee shop all the time. That meant they liked her.

Dad drank lots of rum and Cokes. I'd heard him tell Mom he had stopped drinking, but I knew rum was drinking. I wished I could tell Mom that Dad had lied and was still drinking alcohol. Mom had made a mistake; she couldn't trust him.

Soon, everyone was sleeping except me. I was thinking about Mom and Soling and how worried they must be. I hoped Dad was right and they were on the plane after ours. I wondered if Soling would remember to bring my hula hoop.

I couldn't wait to land so I could see Mom. I knew she would be there because she'd never leave us for long.

Feeling better, I fell asleep.

---

When I woke up, we were still flying. I wondered what Disneyland was like. Mom said we'd gone there when it first opened, but I'd been only four years old at the time. I remembered big cups sitting on saucers that spun around and around. We had pictures of that day.

I wanted Mom to be with us when we went back. She always explained everything and answered all my questions. I wanted to ask her why we'd left the Philippines, why we had to go to America, why she'd taken another plane when there was room on ours. We hadn't even gotten to go swimming.

Surprises are supposed to be fun. This wasn't fun.

I prayed my rosary over and over.

## Chapter 8:

# ON THE MOVE

It was dark when we landed in Los Angeles, and Mom wasn't there to meet us. Where was she? My heart hurt. I felt lost without my mother and just wanted to go home.

"When will Mom get here?" I asked Dad for the hundredth time.

"Her flight was canceled," he said, an angry look on his face. "Stop asking.

I stopped asking and cried inside.

We took a taxi to our auntie Feling and uncle Ted's house. They were Filipino but not our real relatives. Dad said they were good friends of Mom's when we lived in America.

"Can we call Mom when we get to their house?" I asked.

"Don't be stupid, you can't call the Philippines from the United States," he said.

No one ever had called me stupid before, and I knew he was lying because the Americans at our coffee shop called the United States all the time. I was going to tell Dad that, but he warned me not to ask any more questions, or else. *Why does he always say, "or else"?* I wondered.

Los Angeles was a really big town. There were more buildings and cars than I'd ever seen, and the cars all went really fast in the same direction. In the Philippines, you squeezed in where you could because the cars were close together. Our driver back home used his car horn all the time. Dad said cars in America didn't use their horns because of traffic laws. *I guess that's why they go in a straight line*, I thought. Things were so different in Los Angeles. I hoped Mom wouldn't get lost when she came to get us.

When we got to Auntie Feling and Uncle Ted's house, they were surprised and asked where Mom was. I looked at Dad. He told them about the coffee shop and said she would come after she tied up a few loose ends. *What are loose ends?* I knew he'd get mad if I asked, so I decided to wait 'til later and ask Valorie. Valorie knew everything.

Auntie Feling and Uncle Ted were excited when they pulled us into their house. Uncle Ted went straight into the kitchen to fix food; Filipinos always fix food when someone visits. Auntie Feling asked lots of questions about where we'd been, how long were we staying, and what we were doing back in the States—that was short for "United States," I knew that from the coffee shop.

I knew better than to answer any of her questions. Dad did all the talking, even though Auntie Feling was looking at us kids. She asked where our suitcases were. All we had were the plastic bags Mom had packed for us. Dad said the airlines lost our luggage. I wanted to yell that Dad was lying about the suitcases and Mom didn't have to tie loose ends, whatever those were, but instead I kept quiet.

My auntie and uncle had a really big house. Dad called it a California bungalow. The living room was the biggest room, and they had four bedrooms and three bathrooms. We couldn't believe it had three bathrooms. I'd never known anyone with three bathrooms. I didn't know why they had such a big house for the two of them. Maybe they thought they were going to have four children.

Well, now they did.

Auntie Feling and Uncle Ted wanted us to spend the night. They said we all looked tired; Vincent was already asleep on their couch. Dad said okay.

---

That night turned into many nights. I didn't want to leave anyway, not until Mom got there. Dad left us at the house while he went out to look for a job. Uncle Ted let Dad borrow some money, and he promised to pay him back.

My auntie and uncle loved having us, and they said we could stay as long as we wanted. I liked that idea because it was like being home with Mom. Auntie gave each of us fun chores, just like at the coffee shop. She taught Valorie how to use a vacuum machine to clean the rugs, I dusted and made beds, Vance helped Uncle Ted in the garage, and Vincent got to play in the backyard with Champ, a long, skinny dog who Uncle Ted said was a Dachshund.

We shopped at clean inside markets where there were no maids arguing over the price of food. We bought clothes at stores lots of stories high where everything was pretty and neat. America was so different and fun. I wished Mom could see all this. I prayed my rosary extra hard every night, but she still didn't come.

When Dad showed up a couple of weeks later, he told

my auntie and uncle that Mom was having problems with her visa, which meant it was going to take longer than he'd first thought for her to leave the Philippines. But he'd found a job and an apartment close to a school, so we had to leave.

I didn't want to leave, but you never argued with my dad.

The American school was different from my school in Cebu. The kids in the new school didn't wear uniforms. I wished we had uniforms, so I didn't have to wear the two dresses Auntie had bought me over and over. I had two T-shirts and two pairs of shorts at home for playing outside, but I wasn't allowed to wear them to school. The kids in my class noticed that I had only two dresses and a boy called me poor.

Not having lots of clothes didn't make me poor, did it? I thought about it. The begging children in front of Mom's coffee shop were poor, and they hardly had any clothes. I'd felt sorry for those children, but the kids in my class didn't feel sorry for me—they laughed. I wished I was back with my auntie and uncle. I wished I was back at the coffee shop even more.

There was a lady named Miss Theresa, like my middle name, who lived near our apartment. She was nice, and Dad paid her to watch Vincent when I was at school. She took care of other children and had lots of toys. Vincent cried the first day Dad dropped him off, but he didn't after that. I think he liked playing with the other children and the toys. I was so glad he was happy there. I was happy when Vincent was happy.

We'd only been at our new school for a couple of months when Dad picked us up in a blue Cadillac. He said he'd borrowed it from his job selling used cars, and we were going to Colorado.

Where was Colorado?

He drove us straight home, and we packed quickly. It didn't take long, since we only had a few things, but even so Dad kept saying, "Get a move on, we don't have all day!"

Why were we in such a hurry? If we left, would Mom be able to find us?

"Can we stop at Auntie Feling and Uncle Ted's to say good-bye and tell them where we're going?" I asked.

Dad said no. My stomach began to hurt. I wanted them to tell Mom where we were going, so she didn't get lost looking for us. Before we left our auntie's, she'd written to Mom and put a picture of us in the envelope. She'd said it would take twelve weeks for it to reach the Philippines. That was a long time. Now we were leaving, and I wouldn't get to know what Mom wrote back.

I memorized their phone number by heart: DU-1-2409. Auntie made me say it over and over so I wouldn't forget. As soon as someone let me use their phone and Dad wasn't looking, I was going to call them. I wondered if it was a sin not to tell Dad.

I'd made a friend at school named Jean Jones. She was my best friend, and she only had a couple of dresses, too. We'd walk to her house after school, and she'd make us Nestle's Quick with cow's milk. She wore her house key on a chain around her neck like I wore my rosary around mine. She didn't have a mother, but her father was really nice. She told me her mother was never coming back. I told her mine was coming soon. I couldn't wait for Jean to meet my mother, and now she wouldn't be able to. I felt sad about that, and that I didn't have time to say good-bye to my new friend.

The blue Cadillac wasn't new, but it looked new, and it had big seats, perfect for sleeping. When we were done packing, Valorie and Vance sat in the backseat and Vincent sat with me up front.

We drove all night. When we stopped for gas, I asked where Colorado was, but Dad didn't answer me. He just smoked his Salem cigarettes and told us not to bother him. He said he needed to think. Whenever he said stuff like that, you knew not to ask questions.

Valorie and Vance slept huddled together in the backseat to keep warm. Vincent's warm little body was lying across my lap. He was my little heater. Even his breath on my arm was warm. I covered him with my sweater and leaned my shoulder on the door with my head against the window. Every bump on the road woke me up, but I didn't move; I didn't want to wake Vincent. I looked down at his face and touched his soft, chubby cheeks, feeling so much love for him. I'd promised Mom I wouldn't let him out of my sight. I'd promised in God's name. It was a promise I would keep.

Sometimes Vincent called me Mommy; other times he called me Banca, a nickname Soling had given me. (A *banca* is a fishing boat with bamboo sticking out of its sides to keep it from tipping over. Soling said I looked like a *banca* when I was learning to walk because I stuck my arms out to my sides.) At first, I corrected Vincent when he called me Mommy, but I'd gotten tired of doing that every time, so I didn't anymore. I let him call me whatever he wanted.

I was sound asleep when suddenly the car pulled onto a bumpy road. The tires made loud crunching noises for a few seconds before we came to a stop.

It was early in the morning, and I had never been so cold. It didn't get this cold in the Philippines. When Dad turned the car off, the heater went off too. Thank goodness I had my little heater sleeping on my lap.

I was the first one awake. "Where are we?" I asked.

"We're at your grandmother's house in Englewood, Colorado," he said.

"What's her name?" I asked.

"Phyllis Bromley," he said.

I knew we had another grandmother because Mom talked about her a lot. Mom said she was really nice and had taught her how to make the special donuts sprinkled with sugar that the Americans liked so much. I wanted to meet my nice American grandmother, but all I could think about was missing my mother, Soling, Lolo, and Lola. I had that sick feeling in my stomach again.

We were getting farther and farther away from Mom.

## Chapter 9:

# MY OTHER GRANDMA

We were all lined up—Valorie, Veronica, Vance, and Vincent—on Grandma Phyllis's couch. Grandma's house was small and smelled stuffy, but it was warm. It felt good to be out of the Cadillac.

I loved Grandma right away. She asked us to stand up one at a time so she could give each of us a big bear hug. I'd never seen a bear and didn't know they hugged. She asked us if we remembered her. Valorie said she did, but I wasn't sure.

A small brown-and-white dog with short legs came running in to say hello. Grandma said his name was Knees; I told her I didn't know dogs had knees. She said it was short for Pekingese; I thought it must be like States being short for United States.

Grandma also had kittens, and all three of them were on Vance's lap. Cats were Vance's favorite, even though in the Philippines animals were only allowed under the house and mostly they walked around the streets, looking for food.

Grandma Phyllis was taller than any lady I'd ever seen. She was as tall as Dad. She had curly gray hair and a big smiling face and talked very loudly. Dad said it was because Grandma couldn't hear very well. She stood in front of us with her hands on her hips and her feet apart. I looked down at her feet and wondered why she was wearing two different shoes; I'd have to ask her later.

My other grandma, Phyllis Bromley

Grandma wore an apron covered with purple flowers. "Are you hungry?" she asked with a serious face.

We said, "Yes!" all at the same time. Vance and Vincent started bouncing up and down on the couch with excitement, and I whispered, "Remember your manners." They stopped bouncing but kept smiling.

"Do you want eggs and bacon?" Grandma asked.

"Yes, please!" we shouted. You could have heard us down the street,

Then she asked, "Do you kids like biscuits and pancakes?"

We all started clapping and the boys began bouncing up and down again. This was going to be the best breakfast ever.

"Who wants to help me make breakfast?" Grandma Phyllis asked.

We all raised our hands and said we were good helpers. Vincent raised both his hands. I told Grandma how we helped Mom at the coffee shop. She smiled and pulled two aprons out of a drawer. Valorie took the pink one and I got the flowered one like Grandma's.

We followed Grandma into the kitchen like four baby chicks behind their mother and crowded around the warm pot-belly stove in the corner. *What a funny name!* I guessed that it was called that because it looked like it had a big belly. Grandma pulled out bowls and wooden spoons. She talked about our grandpa Earl and how much he'd loved our mother and us kids. I asked where Grandpa Earl was, and Grandma said he'd died. I felt sad when she said that, and even though I didn't remember him I got tears in my eyes, until she said he was looking down on us right now. Then I looked up and smiled at Grandpa Earl.

Dad stayed outside, smoking and looking at a map. He only came in the house to use Grandma's phone and get coffee. He didn't even ask permission.

In no time, Grandma's house smelled like biscuits, bacon, and coffee, which made my stomach growl. It was fun stirring the batter for the pancakes and scrambling the eggs. Vance was in charge of telling Grandma when the coffee pot on the stove started bubbling. When it was time to eat, we gathered around the kitchen table. We'd made so much food, and we couldn't wait to get started.

Grandma went outside to tell Dad breakfast was ready, but he only wanted another cup of coffee, a biscuit, and a pack of cigarettes out of his bag.

When she came back inside, Grandma served each of us a full plate of food. We had scrambled eggs, crispy bacon, biscuits with gravy, and a side of pancakes with lots of butter and syrup. We even had hot chocolate with whipped cream on top. We sat quickly, held hands, and gave thanks for our food, just like Mom taught us. After saying grace, the only sounds you heard were lips smacking and words like "yummy."

Grandma went outside to talk to Dad. "You've got to stop dragging these poor kids all over the country!" I heard her tell him.

How did Grandma know we were poor? I also heard her say "Feling and Ted." Those were my aunt and uncle's names. I was glad she knew our auntie and uncle; maybe she could call them and tell them where we were so Mom could find us. Then I heard Grandma say my mother's name, "Lily."

I wanted to jump up to listen closer but knew better. When Dad was mad, you stayed far away.

Dad raised his voice at Grandma, then came in, grabbed his car keys, and left, slamming the front door behind him. I was glad he was gone. It was always better when he wasn't around.

"Our mother is coming soon," I told Grandma.

She smiled. "I think so too."

My rosary was working. I decided to be patient.

I finally asked Grandma why she wore two different shoes. She said she had a bunion on one foot. "A bump on my big toe," she explained.

I felt sorry for her. "Does it hurt?"

"Scots are tough," she said.

Grandma's name before she married John Slaughter was Phyllis McKay. She told us McKay was a Scottish name, and we were part Scottish. Our ancestors were warriors called Highlanders in Scotland. I remembered Lolo telling me that our four-times great-grandfather was Lapu-Lapu, and he was a warrior too. He killed a Spanish explorer named Ferdinand Magellan, who was trying to take our land. Lolo said it's not a sin if you kill someone protecting yourself. I was a warrior, but I knew I'd never kill anybody.

I don't know how long we stayed with Grandma, but it was more than a few days. I wished we would never leave. My mother could find us if we stayed at Grandma's. I told Grandma Phyllis about Auntie Feling and Uncle Ted in Los Angeles. She said she knew them and would tell them where we were. I believed Grandma and gave her their phone number, DU-1-2409. Grandma told me she'd write to Mom and let her know too. I was so excited! I asked her to tell Mom to come right away and not to forget Soling and to tell her how much we loved and missed her. Grandma Phyllis took a picture of us and said she'd send it to Mom with her letter. This was the first time in months I'd felt happy. I asked Grandma if it was a sin if I didn't tell my dad. She said it wasn't, so I promised in God's name not to mention the letter or the picture.

Grandma Phyllis told us stories about our grandpa Earl. She said Earl was actually our half-grandfather because he wasn't Dad's father. Grandma said our real grandfather was John Slaughter, who died of a heart attack. She said he was an alcoholic and mean. Grandma was surprised that we didn't know Dad had a brother. Uncle John was a year older than Dad, and they didn't get along. Grandma said Dad and Grandpa John were "two of a kind." I asked her what that meant, and she said they were "cut from the same cloth." I didn't understand that either, so I stopped asking.

Earl Bromley was Grandma's second husband. He didn't drink alcohol and was kind. He raised Golden Palomino horses and worked at a rubber factory in Littleton. Grandma said he got cancer from his job. That's a really bad sickness. Grandpa Earl's favorite horse was named Golden Boy; he was Grandpa's pride and joy. I knew what that meant without having to ask Grandma. It's when you loved something that made you very happy. I was sure we were Mom's pride and joy. When we went to the cemetery to visit our Grandpa Earl, there was a picture of Golden Boy on his tombstone. He really did love his horse.

We all cried when Dad said it was time to leave. I heard him arguing with Grandma again in the back room. She came out and said, "Leave the kids with me, Bob."

"No," Dad said, "we're moving to our own place."

I asked Grandma if she was going to visit us. She promised she would. I knew she kept her promises.

Grandma looked like she was crying as she packed our clothes. She was a Scot, and I didn't know if they were supposed to cry; warriors aren't cry babies, after all. Was I really going to see Grandma again? Would Mom get Grandma's letter and come right away? Dad promised we'd be back, but he never kept his promises.

I hoped the next place we went would be a happy place like Grandma's. For the first time, I thought about running away—running back to Grandma's house to wait for Mom. But I couldn't leave Vincent, he was too little. I knew when babies don't have their mothers, they die. I wasn't going to let Vincent die. Mom had told me to watch after him, and I'd promised in the name of God that I would.

After bear hugs and kisses from Grandma, we slowly climbed back into the blue Cadillac. Valorie sat up front with Dad this time, and the boys sat with me in the back. I waved to Grandma as we backed down the rocky driveway. It reminded me of waving to Mom the last time I saw her. I pulled Vincent close and wondered what was next.

I held my rosary tight.

Chapter 10:

# ST. CLARA'S

After leaving Grandma Phyllis's house, we moved to a small apartment in Denver. I don't remember much about the apartment because we weren't there long, but Grandma came to visit like she'd promised. We jumped up and down with excitement when we opened the door and saw her standing there. She gave us big bear hugs and brought us a children's book and bag of her yummy donuts sprinkled with sugar. I wanted to go with her for a few days since we were out of school for the summer.

"If we go with Grandma, you won't have to find a babysitter for us when you're at work," I told Dad. I was crossing my fingers behind my back, hoping he would say yes. I felt safe at Grandma's house.

Dad didn't answer me, but he called Grandma into our only bedroom. Dad slept on the couch and the four of us slept in one bed. We looked like sardines in a can, lined up next to each other. I loved sardines.

Grandma pulled a letter from her purse and told Dad she had news. He closed the bedroom door, but I could still hear Grandma's loud voice. I heard her mention Mom's name and the Philippines. Then she said something about "Lily's rights" and "the children."

After only a few minutes, Dad yelled, "Stay out of my business!" and stomped out of the room. He was so angry, his face was red. We hurriedly moved out of his way.

When Grandma came out of the room, she was still holding the letter. Dad tried to grab it, but she wouldn't give it to him. He told Grandma to leave and pointed to the door. Then he looked at us and said, "You're not going anywhere with this woman."

*What does he mean, "this woman"?* She was our grandma, and we wanted to go with her. My stomach started hurting bad, and I don't think it was because we'd eaten all the sugary donuts and hadn't saved any for Dad.

While Grandma was giving me a good-bye bear hug, she whispered in my ear, "Call me if you move. I wrote my phone number in the back of the book I gave you." Then she kissed the top of my head.

We all begged Grandma not to go. She told us things were going to be better soon and not to worry. The letter must have had something to do with Mom. Maybe she was on her way to get us. I ran over to Vincent and gave him the biggest bear hug I could, then prayed my rosary.

---

A few days after Grandma's visit, Dad took us for a drive. I asked where we were going but all he said was, "You'll see." I was hoping we were going to Grandma's house; she didn't live far. Instead, we stopped in front of two huge iron gates with a driveway that led to the biggest house I'd ever seen. We drove slowly up the driveway, passing nice trees on both sides, until we reached the large front door. There was a giant white statue of an angel; one of her hands was pointing up toward heaven, and the other was resting on the shoulder of a small child.

Driveway to St. Clara

"Stay in the car," Dad said as he got out.

I wondered if this house was haunted like the ones I saw on television. Valorie said it was a mansion, which meant a really big house, and it couldn't be haunted because it had an angel out front. Who would live in a house like this and why were we here? Did Dad know the people who lived here?

He walked up to the large wooden doors and knocked loudly. A nun dressed all in black opened one of the doors. She put her hand out to Dad, but I couldn't hear what she was saying, so I rolled down the window and leaned out as far as I could. I still couldn't hear.

She looked like the nuns in the Philippines, except much taller. Why were Americans so tall!? The nun at the door also had a long rosary hanging from her waist, just like the nuns in the Philippines. I wished I had a rosary like that. Mom said nuns were kind and loving because they were brides of God. Maybe this place was a Catholic school! *Are we going to change schools again? Will we get to wear uniforms?*

Dad came back to the car and told us we were having lunch with the nuns. He said they were from Belgium. I'd never heard of Belgium and wondered why we were having lunch with them. *Maybe these kind nuns will help us find Mom.*

As I started to open the car door, Dad stopped me. "Do not talk about the past; do not mention your mother or the Philippines. Do you understand?"

He looked mad, so we just nodded up and down. Now I was worried. Why did he say that? I wanted to ask these nice nuns if they knew nuns in the Philippines. I was sure all nuns knew each other, because they were sisters, and you always talked to your sisters.

"I told the nuns you're all adopted," Dad said.

"What does adopted mean?" I asked.

"It's when an adult takes care of someone else's children," he said. "It's important that you don't tell the nuns anything else."

Why couldn't we tell the nuns that we were his children? Why did we have to lie? You weren't supposed to lie to nuns.

The four of us walked into the giant brick house holding hands. Dad introduced us to the nun who'd answered the door, her name was Sister Daniels. I wondered why brides of God never had babies.

We followed Sister Daniels into a room that looked like a library. There, we sat quietly at a long wooden table and waited. Valorie was smiling because there were hundreds of books around us. She loved to read. She even read newspapers after other people were finished with them.

I wasn't smiling. The smell in the room was making me feel sick in my stomach. I wished they would open one of the big windows so I could breathe.

A teenage girl came into the room with sandwiches and milk. She put the plates on the table and left the room without saying hello or even looking at us. I wasn't hungry, so I pushed my sandwich toward Vance; he was always hungry.

Sister Daniels looked at me. "We don't waste food here!" She seemed mad.

I wanted to say I wasn't wasting food; I was sharing it with my brother. Instead, I kept quiet.

Another nun walked in, smiling. "My name is Sister Mary Joseph. What are your names?"

Before I could answer, Dad stared at me with his mean face. I knew I better not mess up.

⁂

When lunch was over, I couldn't wait to get out of there. No matter what Valorie said, this place felt like a haunted house to me. Sister Daniels wasn't nice like the nuns in the Philippines, she looked mean. I stood up and was ready to leave when Dad said, "I have to go away for a few days and want you to stay with these nice nuns."

Sister Daniels stood with her arms crossed and her eyebrows squished together. Her hands disappeared into the sleeves of her long-sleeved robe. I wondered if she was hiding a switch or paddle in her big sleeves.

I put my arm around Vincent. I wanted to scream, "Don't leave us here!" but instead I asked. "Why can't we go with you?"

"Because I'm having surgery," he said.

I didn't know Dad was sick. "Can we go to Grandma's?" I asked.

He turned and looked at me with his angry face. I must have said something wrong.

"I won't be gone long," Dad said. "And you will be well taken care of here."

Now I was really scared, because he never told the truth. I wanted to call my grandma, but I didn't have the book she'd given us with her phone number in it. Dad told the nuns he'd bring our clothes the next day, and I hoped he wouldn't forget the book from Grandma.

We all cried as he got ready to leave. Valorie held onto Dad's waist and wouldn't let go.

"You're my *big girl*," he said. "I'm counting on you to look after your brothers and sister."

Why was this happening? I wanted to tell the nuns we had a mother and we weren't adopted. I wanted to tell them our father was lying, and they should call our grandmother. I took my rosary out of my pocket and put it around my neck.

Dad never did come back with our things.

---

The first month at St. Clara's Orphanage was like a nightmare I couldn't wake up from. The worst part was that they took Vincent away from me. There wasn't anything I could say to make them understand that I was his mother.

Sister Daniels was the meanest of all the nuns. You could never see her eyes because she wore thick, dark glasses all the time. She made Vance live in the building next to ours because he was considered one of the *big boys*, even though he was only seven. Boys seven to seventeen lived in a different building than the girls. I prayed to God not let them separate us, but God didn't hear me.

Valorie and I were on the girls' side, so we were together. The big girls and little girls slept on the same floor. When you turned eighteen, you had to leave the orphanage; I wished I was eighteen instead of nine. A few girls stayed after they turned eighteen and worked for the nuns, like the one who'd served us sandwiches on our first day.

Vincent was on the floor beneath us with the *little boys*, boys six and under. I was glad Vincent was four.

I missed Vance a lot. Sometimes when the big boys were in the play yard out back, I could see him through the tall wire fence separating the girls from the boys. I hated that fence. When I spotted Vance on the other side, I'd wave my arms until they hurt. The nuns didn't like us talking at the fence, so I threw him kisses. He never smiled; he just looked at me with his arms at his side and cried. He wasn't the silly, happy little boy he'd once been anymore.

I looked for Vance at Sunday Mass, too. The boys and girls sat on different sides of the church. Even when I did see him, I couldn't hug him or even say hi.

I thanked God that he'd let Valorie, Vincent, and me live in the same building. I prayed my rosary more at St. Clara's Orphanage than I ever had anywhere else.

There were hundreds of children at St. Clara's. None of them had parents, and they were called orphans. We weren't orphans! We had a mother and father and didn't belong there. Dad had said not to talk about our past, but I told anyone who would listen about my mother and how she was on her way to get us. I didn't bother making friends at St. Clara's because I thought I wasn't going to be there long.

I was wrong.

Days turned into months at the orphanage. Everyone had daily chores. The older you were, the harder your chores. If you didn't finish on time, you were punished by not getting dinner—or, worse, getting hit with a wooden paddle.

Valorie's job was cleaning the giant marble stairs that went from the first floor to the second floor. There were so many stairs, Valorie worried she wouldn't finish. I wanted to help her when I was done with my chores, but I knew we'd both get punished if we were caught. I prayed she'd finish on time.

She was supposed to do one stair at a time: wash with soap, rinse, then dry each stair. Valorie thought it would be faster if she washed three stairs at a time, then rinsed them, then went back to dry them. Her plan was working well until one day, Sister Daniels started down the stairs after Valorie had just washed three stairs, and she almost slipped on one of them. She got angry and hit Valorie so hard she tumbled down the marble stairs.

When Valorie stood up, her mouth was bleeding. Sister Daniels didn't even say she was sorry. Valorie was sent to the infirmary, where she got stitches inside and outside of her mouth. The infirmary was like a hospital, and she spent the night there and ate ice cream and Jell-O for dinner. The nun in the infirmary was the smiling nun, Sister Mary Joseph. She was nice like the nuns in the Philippines.

My job was to help the little girls shower and dress before breakfast. The shower room was one big room for all the girls. If anyone took off their underwear in the shower room, they would get in trouble. You had to soap inside your underwear and then rinse. When you finished washing, you went into a small dressing room where you'd take your wet underwear off and put on your dry underwear. Every girl had two pairs of underwear with their names on them. My job was to make sure the dirty ones went in the hamper and the clean ones were folded and placed on their marked shelf. Anyone caught naked had to go to Sister Daniel's office. She'd pull your underwear down and hit your bare bottom till it had red bumps.

None of the little girls I helped ever got a spanking. I wished Vincent was a little girl so I could take care of him.

The big girls' dorm had five rows of ten beds. The beds were close together, with just enough room between them to kneel for prayers. We prayed first thing in the morning and before bed at night. My bed was right under a big round window. I could see the moon and stars at night before going to sleep. It was the only time I was happy at St. Clara's.

⁂

One night, I woke up to someone trying to get into my bed. I felt a hot little body and realized it was my little heater. I had shown Vincent where I slept when we'd first arrived at St. Clara's. My bed was the only one under the big round window. Vincent had remembered and found me. Crying softly, he told me he'd wet his bed.

"I don't want to get another spanking," he whispered, and then he hugged me real tight. "Can I sleep with you?"

"Don't worry," I said, "everything is going to be okay."

After we hugged each other for a few minutes, I told Vincent it was almost morning and we'd both get in big trouble if we got caught, so we had to hurry. Sister Daniels came in every morning at 6:00 a.m. sharp: *Clap! Clap! Clap!* At the end of third clap you'd better be out of your bed and kneeling next to it with your hands together and head bowed, or you wouldn't get breakfast.

I only had a few minutes to change Vincent's sheets, put clean underwear and pajamas on him, and hurry back to my bed. The nuns would never let me see Vincent again if they found out I'd helped him, but he was my most important job and I had to protect him. I'd promised Mom.

I grabbed Vincent's hand and we dashed downstairs. We were barefoot, so no one could hear us as we ran. I knew where everything was since I was in charge of laundry. I pulled Vincent's sheets off his bed, cleaned him up, and then put clean underwear and pajamas on him. I quickly put the soiled sheets and clothes at the bottom of the big hamper. I would make sure to pick them up first thing in the morning and bring them straight to the laundry building.

I stayed an extra second to tuck Vincent into bed and give him a kiss. "Don't wet your bed," I told him, "but if you do, don't cry, just come get me."

He kept saying he was sorry. I told him everything was alright, and I'd see him at breakfast. He smiled and gave me one last bear hug, and then I ran back upstairs—and arrived just in the nick of time.

My heart was pounding, but I was smiling as I bowed my head into my hands for morning prayers. I'd outsmarted the mean Sister Daniels.

---

Dad came back months later to get us.

Vance wasn't the same after our stay at St. Clara's. He was quiet and kept to himself. The goofy brother with non-stop energy was gone. Vincent, meanwhile, clung to me more than ever. He'd even sit by the bathroom door until I came out. Valorie had a permanent scar under her bottom lip and started keeping a diary to write about her feelings. As for me, I showered with my underwear on for a long time. I felt unwanted, unclean, and unloved.

After our stay at St. Clara's Orphanage, I also decided to call my father by his first name.

He wasn't my dad anymore. He was just Bob.

## Chapter 11:

# WHERE IS MOMMY?

Vincent was pulling on my shirt. "Mommy, Mommy!" he whined.

"I'm not your Mommy!" I yelled.

He stared at me. I couldn't tell if he was going to cry or just stand there with his mouth open. It had been a long time since we'd left the Philippines; I'm not sure how long, but it felt like my whole life.

I was tired of being responsible for my little brother. I loved Vincent, but I wasn't his mommy. I didn't want to play Go Fish or hide-and-seek with him anymore. He was almost five and needed to learn to play by himself. When I didn't feel like playing, he'd walk away with his head down and then sit by himself and cry. I felt bad when he did that, and remembered my promise to Mom, so I'd go and bear hug him, he'd give me a big smile, and then we'd play Go Fish. He didn't know I needed a mommy too.

After St. Clara's, we moved into an apartment building that had a lot of floors. The elevator was always broken, so we had to carry our groceries up three flights of stairs. We practiced holding our breath as we ran up the stairs because it smelled bad in the stairwell. I was glad we didn't live on the top floor.

"Where is Mommy?" I asked Bob every day. "When are she and Soling coming?"

His answer was always the same: "Soon." He said Mom had a lot of important things to do. I knew that couldn't be true because Mom always said there was nothing more important than her *ma nga bata*, her babies. I wasn't a baby anymore, but I liked it when she said that.

I knew Mom was looking for us, and I couldn't understand why she hadn't found us yet. Maybe it was because we kept moving all the time. Was Bob telling her where we were? Was he telling Grandma Phyllis? The last time I asked about Mom, he'd told me Lolo was sick and Mom couldn't leave until he got better. Was he lying? You never knew with Bob. He didn't keep his promises or tell the truth. I didn't believe anything he said.

I wrote many letters to Mom, and Bob promised to mail them, but now I thought he lied about that too. I wanted to call Grandma Phyllis to ask if Mom was sending me letters to her house, but Bob said Grandma's phone wasn't working. Why didn't he want Grandma to know where we were? I knew if Mom had our address, she would come right away, I was sure of it. Without Grandma Phyllis, who was going to help me find Mom? Bob said Auntie Feling's number was disconnected. He dialed DU-1-2409 and handed me the phone. I didn't hear anything; it didn't even ring.

I knew better than to ask about Mom too much. If I asked more than once a day, Bob yelled at me. I hated it when he yelled, but I wasn't afraid of him anymore. Mom never yelled. I had to figure out a way to find our mother. I decided the best thing was to continue praying my rosary every night; I was sure God would hear me. But a lot of people prayed, and he had many prayers to answer. Mom said God heard everyone and fixed everything, so I just had to be patient. I wished he would hurry up and get to me.

Valorie cooked most of the time because she liked it, but once in a while she'd tell me it was my turn to cook. I was good at making grilled cheese sandwiches and hot chocolate. They were my favorite; I made them every time it was my turn. I sure wasn't going to open a can of Chef Boyardee again. Bob always bought that; I didn't know why, because none of us liked it.

For the hot chocolate, I'd put powdered milk in hot water and add Nestles Quick. My friend Jean Jones had taught me how to do this. It was the only way I could get Vincent to drink powdered milk. When the grilled cheese sandwiches were done, we all sat down to eat. We never waited for Bob because he came home at different times and sometimes not at all.

---

One evening, just as we were sitting down at the table to eat our grilled cheese sandwiches with hot chocolate, Bob walked through the front door. Valorie and Vance jumped up and ran to him. He hugged them, which was a good sign. We never knew what kind of mood Bob was going to be in, but if he hugged us it meant he'd had a good day. If he threw his keys on the floor and walked funny, we'd go to our room and wait until he fell asleep on the couch before coming out. Tonight, Bob walked in with a big smile on his face and said, "Good news, I got a job!"

We clapped because we knew that meant we would have money soon.

Bob also had a big bag of groceries with him. That was the best present ever. We ripped open the bag and pulled out a gallon of real milk, bread, eggs, cinnamon rolls, hot dogs, Kraft Mac & Cheese, and Oreo cookies. There was also Kool-Aid and a six-pack of Pabst Blue Ribbon beer. I was so glad he hadn't bought any Chef Boyardee.

Bob sat with us at the table. "Bring me a beer, Vance." He never said please.

I made him a grilled cheese sandwich, then sat down across from him.

"I got a job selling new cars," he said between bites of his sandwich.

I wondered if that meant we were going to give back the blue Cadillac and get a new one.

"I'll have to work every day, including weekends," he said. Then he instructed Valorie and Vance to come straight home from school from then on. He told me I still couldn't go to school until he got his first check to pay a babysitter for Vincent. My job was my little brother, but I already knew that. He reminded us not to talk to the neighbors or leave the apartment; he didn't want anyone to know we were home alone, he said, because if people found out he'd get in trouble, and the police would come and take us away. We would be separated and put in different foster homes. As far as I could tell, a foster home was like being adopted. All I really knew was that it meant being separated, like the nuns had done to us at St. Clara's, and I'd rather have died than go through that again.

There was a lady downstairs named Carla who knew I didn't go to school. She had a cute baby who couldn't walk yet. Once in a while, Carla would have a man come to visit her; she had lots of men friends. When her friend came, she would bring the baby upstairs and ask me to watch him for a while and sometimes she'd give me money. I knew Carla wouldn't tell anyone I was home with Vincent because I was her friend and she liked me. She even gave me a necklace with a little pearl at the end of it. I treasured that necklace. I never told Bob about the baby because I wasn't supposed to talk to the neighbors. I was glad he'd finally gotten a job; I wanted to go back to school.

While Bob was finishing his grilled cheese sandwich and opening his second beer with a church key—*that name made no sense at all*—I got the courage to ask about Mom again. "Have you heard from Lolo. Is he better? Is he going to let Mom come to the United States now?"

Bob stared at me for a very long time. I couldn't tell if he was thinking or about to yell at me. I felt nervous but I needed to know. Having Mom with us was the only way the pain in my stomach would go away.

Then Bob bowed his head like he was praying. We all stopped chewing and held our breath. Vincent got up from his chair to stand close to me. We didn't know what Bob was going to do next. Then he did something we never expected: with his head still bowed, he started crying, sobbing.

None of us had ever seen our father cry before. We looked at each other and didn't know what to do or say. Bob's shoulders started moving up and down as he cried. I didn't feel sorry for him, I felt confused.

"Why is Daddy crying?" Vincent whispered.

I put my finger on his lips. "Shhhh."

After crying for a long time, Bob stopped long enough to looked up and stare straight at me. His eyes looked sad, but I didn't see any tears. "I've tried to keep this from you children, because I knew how painful this would be, but the plane your mother and Soling were on . . . crashed."

"What does that mean?" I shouted. "Where are Mommy and Soling now?" I held my breath.

He inhaled extra slow. "In heaven."

I froze. I covered my ears with my hands and started screaming at the top of my lungs with my eyes squeezed tight. Valorie started crying quietly. Vance was crying because Valorie was crying.

The only person not crying was Vincent. My baby brother was hugging me and running his little hand up and down my back. And he was doing his best to make me feel better when he said, "Everything is going to be okay, Mommy."

I turned and pushed him away as hard as I could. "I'm not your mommy! Your mommy is dead!"

Now Vincent was crying too. I ran to the bathroom and locked the door.

After crying until I had no tears left, I told myself, *Bob's lying! He must be lying. He has been lying this whole time! He lied when we left the Philippines, he lied to our auntie and uncle, he lied to Grandma Phyllis, he lied to the nuns, and he is lying now.* I just had to keep praying and trusting God.

When I finally came out of the bathroom, Bob was gone. I washed my face and then went to find Vincent. He was hiding behind the couch.

"I'm sorry," I said softly. "Can I have a bear hug?"

He slowly crawled out, and we hugged each other tight.

I prayed my rosary twice that night as I held Vincent close to me. I knew in my heart that my mother wasn't dead, and no one could tell me different.

My stomach stopped hurting. I stopped crying. I had to wait. I had to be patient. She would come. God would make sure she found us.

I never asked Bob about Mom again.

## Chapter 12:

# BLONDES HAVE MORE FUN

One morning, as I stood at the kitchen sink doing dishes, I felt Bob standing behind me. After what seemed forever, I turned around.

"Do you need something?" I asked, thinking, *What did I do wrong this time?*

He looked me up and down, turned me around, and said, "You have dishwater-blond hair, Veronica."

I stared at him without saying a word. Once again, I had no idea what Bob was talking about. Dishwater was brownish, smelly, and ugly. I looked down into the sink of dirty dishes and wondered why he was saying that. I was ten years old and still confused by the things he said. I wanted to be strong, so I held back my tears; I never wanted anyone to see me cry, especially Bob. People picked on you when you cried. Bob said crying was for sissies.

"I'm taking you to see a friend of mine named Bridget," he said. "She owns the beauty shop where I get my hair cut.

I'm going to ask her to dye your dirty-blond hair. It might help you look prettier."

Now I was concerned. I'd never thought of my long brown hair as "dirty." Since living at St. Clara's, I'd gotten into the habit of washing and scrubbing my hair and skin daily, sometimes twice. The Belgian nuns said, "Cleanliness is next to Godliness," and I wanted to please God.

I didn't want to dye my hair, but I didn't want to be ugly, either, so off to the beauty salon we went. It turned out that Bob liked the hairdresser. He winked at her and called her beautiful, and she was. Bridget had short blond hair and pretty white teeth. I had spaces between my teeth and sometimes Vance called me "Beaver." I wished I looked like the pretty hairdresser.

"Why do you want to dye her hair?" Bridget asked.

"She wants to be a blonde," Bob lied. "Blondes have more fun, don't they?" he said, grinning.

I wanted to have more fun. I smiled at Bridget. "Is that true?"

She patted the chair and I jumped up. "I don't want dishwater- or dirty-blond hair anymore," I said. "I want to be a pretty blonde like you."

She smiled. "You're already pretty."

I looked over at Bob, hoping he'd heard Bridget, but he wasn't listening; he was staring at the pretty hairdresser's legs.

I sat in Bridget's chair for hours. I didn't know being a blonde took so much time. She put stuff on my head that smelled and burned my scalp and eyes. I wanted to tell her to stop but it was too late; my hair was white after she stripped my color. She said stripping was necessary if I wanted to be a blonde.

I looked uglier every time I opened my eyes and looked in the mirror in front of me. She kept saying, "We're almost finished."

When she was finally done, my hair was yellow. It didn't look anything like hers. I hated it but didn't want to hurt her feelings. Tears started to fill my eyes.

"What's wrong, sweetie?" Bridget asked.

"The stuff you put on my head is still burning my eyes," I lied, wiping my eyes.

Why had I gone through all this? The only thing I liked was my haircut; it was a pageboy like hers. I didn't think being a blonde made me look any prettier. I thanked her anyway, because she'd worked a long time at trying to make me look better. I wished she had dyed my hair black like my mother's. My mother was prettier than anyone I'd ever seen.

"Her hair looks great," Bob said. "She's almost as beautiful as you."

Bridget ignored Bob. I was glad. I don't think she liked Bob very much; she seemed to like me more. She talked to me the whole time I was in her chair and kept giving me little hugs on my shoulders. He asked her out to dinner, but she still didn't say much—just said she had plans that night without even looking at him. He asked her about the next day. She didn't answer again. That's what Bob did to me when I asked him questions; now he knew how it felt.

Bridget helped me out of the chair and had me look at the back of my head with a mirror I held in my hand. She hugged me again, and then Bob handed her some money.

"Thanks," she said. "You have a beautiful daughter."

He didn't say a word, and he didn't talk to me all the way home.

◆●◆

When we got back to the apartment, Bob said my hair had cost him an arm and leg and he hadn't even gotten to first base.

Everything was always my fault. First base must mean a date, and I didn't think you could buy an arm or leg. I hated my hair. Blondes didn't have more fun. I wanted my dishwater hair back.

I had just started back to school after taking care of Vincent for a month while Bob looked for a job and then got his first paycheck. I didn't want to go to school with my yellow hair; I was sure I'd be made fun of by the other kids. Now what was I going to do?

I thought about wearing the scarf Bob had brought home a few weeks ago. It smelled like perfume; one of his girlfriends had probably left it in his car. In the end, though, I decided to stay home. I told Bob I didn't feel well and would stay home and watch Vincent. It wasn't really a lie, because the thought of going to school with yellow hair made my stomach hurt.

Now that Bob was working, Carla downstairs watched Vincent while I was in school. She didn't have her friends visit so much anymore and when I asked her why, she said they weren't really friends. I knew what she meant; I didn't have any real friends either.

After Bob left for work, I took Vincent downstairs to tell Carla she didn't have to take care of my brother because I would be home with him that day. When she opened the door, she looked surprised.

"What happened to your beautiful hair?" she asked, a frown on her face.

As soon as she said that, I started crying and couldn't stop. I tried to hide my tears, but it was impossible. I told her a pretty hairdresser did this to me because Bob hated my dishwater-blond hair. He said blondes had more fun.

Carla held me and said Bob was wrong—that my hair was beautiful, and she would fix everything. I stopped crying but continued to hug her. Vincent hugged her too.

"Lady Clairol will help us," Carla said.

"Is Lady Clairol your hairdresser?" I asked.

She laughed, went into the bathroom, and brought out a box that said Lady Clairol Golden Brown. I liked the sound of Golden-Brown hair!

"This is the hair dye I use," she told me. Her hair was pretty! I was excited—but I hoped being Golden Brown wasn't going to take all day like being a blonde had. I needed to be home before Bob, or I'd get in trouble.

"I don't have any money," I said, "but I'll babysit for you whenever you need me."

She kissed me. "It's a present," she said. "And don't worry, it will only take an hour."

I stopped worrying and knew Carla was going to make everything better. It felt like I had a mother taking care of me.

An hour later, I looked beautiful. My hair looked prettier than ever. I hugged Carla tight before hurrying back upstairs with Vincent.

---

When Bob got home, he asked when I was going back to school. I told him I was feeling better and would go back the next day. I waited for him to yell at me for changing the color of my hair after he'd spent so much money on it, but he didn't say anything.

By the end of the evening, I realized Bob hadn't even noticed the change in my hair. He ignored me most of the time, and tonight I was glad for that.

Whenever Bob talked about how I looked, it made me feel bad inside. I was sure he did it on purpose, probably because I was the only one who didn't run to him for hugs and kisses. When I was sad, I'd picture Soling holding my face and telling me how beautiful I was. She always said I was the most beautiful girl in the Philippines, and Mom would sometimes tell her that I was too smart for my own good. I think that meant I was good and smart. Bob couldn't take the memories in my head away from me.

Late one night, Bob told us we had to pack up right away and leave our apartment. I hated leaving Carla and the baby. I loved her. She was my friend, and I felt safe having her downstairs. I didn't even get a chance to say good-bye or tell her how much I would miss her and the baby.

After we left, I wore the necklace with the pearl that she'd given me, and I thought about her every time I looked at it. I included her in my prayers, along with all the other people I loved.

Once again, we drove all night. This time, we woke up in a city called Las Vegas. It was like no city we had ever driven through. There were twinkly lights everywhere, like it was Christmas. I especially liked the giant cowboy with his arm going back and forth, like he was hitchhiking, and saying, "Howdy Partner." How did they make his arm do that? How did they get him to talk at the same time? The cowboy was covered in red and blue lights, from his cowboy hat to his boots, and had a big cigarette hanging out of his mouth. Every street we drove down had twinkly lights on both sides spelling out names like Flamingo (that one was covered in purple and pink twinkly lights) and the Golden Nugget (that one had millions of bright yellow twinkly lights). Some flashed off and on together and others went off and on one at a time.

Las Vegas was beautiful! And all the restaurants were noisy and had machines that spilled money when you pulled the handle at their sides. This town looked like fun! Bob could make lots of money here!

## CHAPTER 13:

# COLLATERAL DAMAGE

After staying in a hotel with no twinkly lights, we moved into another apartment. I wasn't sure if this was the fifth or sixth place we'd lived in; all I knew was that we had lived in California, then Colorado, and now Nevada. Thank goodness God could see us wherever we were. God sees everything.

Bob met a lady named Sally Doll who lived in a nice house not far from us. She was a dancer and worked at night. When Bob started going out with her, I babysat her six-year-old son Greg, and she paid me. He was easy because all he did was watch TV. While he watched TV, I read the books in his room. Greg was lucky! He had so many games, toys, and books, and a closet full of clothes—it all seemed like a lot for one little boy. And he wasn't even nice to his mother; he talked back to and even yelled at Sally sometimes. I would never have talked like that to my mother.

On the weekends, we all spent the night at Sally's house. She gave us lots of blankets and pillows, and the five of us kids slept on the floor. It was a lot of fun! We stayed up late watching TV and eating Jiffy Pop popcorn. Bob slept in Sally's room.

Sally was the nicest lady. She promised she'd teach me to dance someday. If I could dance like Sally, I thought, maybe Bob would think I was pretty too. Bob liked Sally and was always hugging and kissing her. I asked Bob if we could go with him to watch Sally dance, but he said no, it was for adults only.

Adults had all the fun.

Once, instead of paying me for babysitting, Sally bought me a beautiful green dress. I could hardly remember when I'd last had a new dress. Most of our clothes were from Goodwill. I liked shopping there, though. It was fun looking through all the racks of clothes, and if you searched hard enough, you could find nice clothes without holes or stains.

Now I had a dress that no one had ever worn but me. It had a petticoat under the skirt; it was kind of itchy, but it made the bottom of the dress stand out. I looked like a princess. Sally pulled my hair back with a shiny green ribbon and even put pink lipstick on my lips and pink nail polish on my fingernails. She told me she'd always wanted a girl.

I couldn't wait to show Bob. I wanted him to see that I was pretty. Sally said we'd surprise him when he came to pick me up.

When Bob finally arrived, I was hiding in the kitchen. Sally had said she would tell me when to come out.

I heard Vincent's voice first. He was looking for me, and I hoped he wouldn't ruin the surprise. Then Sally said, "And here is your beautiful princess." That was my signal to make my grand entrance.

I twirled my way out of the kitchen. The itchy petticoat made my dress full; I did feel like a princess. Vincent ran to me. I tried to keep him away, but he threw his arms around my waist and told me I was pretty.

"What do you think of your beautiful daughter, Bob?" Sally asked.

He just stared at me as I was pushing Vincent away. Then he said, "If you want to get a man, Veronica, just lift that dress to your chin. It will make up for not being pretty."

Sally hit Bob in the arm. "Don't say that."

I didn't know what he meant, but I was sure he didn't like the dress and thought I looked stupid. I ran to Greg's room and ripped my brand-new dress trying to take it off. I wiped off the pink lipstick and lay on Greg's bed. I hated myself. I hated Bob. I wished I was invisible.

Vincent climbed up next to me and snuggled into me. Holding Vincent was all I needed. He thought I was pretty with or without a new dress.

I heard Sally and Bob arguing. She seemed mad.

"If you like her so damn much, why don't you keep her!" Bob yelled. I think he had been drinking, because I had never heard him yell at Sally before. I don't know why, but I was happy when he said Sally should keep me. Maybe Vincent and I could stay with Sally Doll. Maybe Sally would help me find my mother.

Then I heard Bob say, "What is she worth to you?"

---

The next day, Sally asked me if I'd like to come live with her.

"You'd have your own room and a lot of pretty dresses," she said. "Your dad has his hands full with four children."

I knew Bob didn't like me, so why not live with Sally? She liked me. "Can Vincent live with us too?" I asked.

"He can visit as much as he'd like, but I'm sorry, he can't live with us, he's too young," she said. "I'll need you to watch Greg when I go to work at night."

I wasn't sure what to do. I wanted to be away from Bob, but not my brothers and sister. "I don't know . . ."

"Just think about it," she told me.

⁂

One night, when Bob came to pick me up from watching Greg, I heard him talking to Sally in the kitchen. He was asking her if he could borrow some money. He needed a lot of money.

"When will you pay me back?" she asked.

"I'll leave Veronica with you as collateral," Bob said.

I wished I knew what that word meant.

Then I heard Sally ask if she could adopt me. She told Bob he wouldn't have to pay her back if she could have me. I remembered that "adopt" meant to take care of a child that wasn't your own. Bob said yes, and I was glad he thought it was okay for me to stay with Sally for a while. I was still confused about the *collateral* part, though, and started to have that sick feeling in my stomach.

I liked Sally. She was pretty and gave me nice things. When I spent the night, she'd let Greg and me have chocolate Maypo for breakfast in the mornings. She'd also bought me a pair of black patent leather shoes, like the pair I'd had in the Philippines. I'd worn those shoes to church every Sunday with Mom. Mom said black patent leather shoes made any outfit look special. I missed my mother.

⁂

One night when we were all at Sally's, Bob came into the living room and told us it was time to go, except I was to stay behind. "I'll come back for you soon," he said.

I remembered him saying the same thing when he left us at St. Clara's. Sally's house was much nicer than St. Clara's, though, and I felt safe there. I decided I did want to stay.

Vincent wanted to stay with me, but Bob told Valorie to take him to the car. Vincent reached his arms toward me, and for a moment I thought I should go, but Bob said I had to stay.

I belonged to Sally now. I had my own room, with pink everything: pink bedspread, pink pillows, and a pink lamp with a ballerina on it. You could wind the lamp up and the ballerina would dance under the lampshade. Sally kissed me every night before bed, just like Mom did. I had everything I could possibly want, but I didn't feel happy. Why? I continued to pray my rosary every night before going to sleep.

Sally's house was nice. I felt loved when I was with her. We ate lots of good food and I never had to cook or clean. She took me shopping at Sears, not the Salvation Army or Goodwill. She bought me underwear, socks, shirts, skirts, and shorts. I'd never had so many clothes. My new underwear came in different colors and had a different day of the week written on the back of each of them. I didn't have to share with Valorie anymore. I remembered when we lived in the apartment where Carla and the baby lived, I once put a pair of my underwear on Vincent because his was in the laundry. He liked them and said they felt silky; we laughed, and it became our secret. I'm sure Bob would have gotten angry if he knew Vincent had worn a pair of girls' underwear.

⁂

I had fun at Sally Doll's house but missed Vincent. After what seemed like a really long time, I started asking Sally if my brothers and sister could come over.

"You said Vincent could visit as much as he wanted," I reminded her. "Can he come over soon?"

"Sure," she said, "but not today."

I hadn't seen them for most of the summer. I worried she wasn't telling the truth. I started asking about my brothers and sister the way I used to ask Bob about Mom and Soling. It didn't feel good. My stomach was starting to hurt all the time.

---

When summer was over and I went back to school, it had been almost two months since I had seen Valorie, Vance, and Vincent. On my first day, I wore an orange-and-white-flowered blouse and an orange pleated skirt with white shoes. I couldn't wait to show Valorie. I looked everywhere for Vance and Valorie but couldn't find them. I was hoping to at least be with them during school.

I asked around about the Slaughter kids. One girl asked me if I meant the fat, ugly girl who looked Chinese. She asked if that was my sister, then made a face and said, "Yuck, Fat Val is your sister?"

I found myself saying, "No, she's not my sister, but I need to talk to her." I was embarrassed of my sister because no one liked her. I was one of the popular girls. I had been invited to birthday parties during the summer by girls in my class. I liked being popular and not feeling stupid or ugly. Kids were treating me like they treated the other rich girls. I had nice clothes and didn't have to wear the same dress over and over. Sally always made sure my clothes matched, my socks were white, and my shoes weren't scuffed up. My sister and I didn't look alike, and I wondered if the other kids didn't like her because she looked Filipino or because she didn't have nice clothes.

I felt bad inside for saying Valorie wasn't my sister and asked God to forgive me for lying. I didn't want to be a liar like Bob. My heart was pounding as I ran around the playground looking for them. *Did Bob move them to another school? Why didn't he come get me? Is he going to leave me with Sally forever? I made a mistake choosing to live with Sally. St Jude, please help me.*

I finally found Valorie and Vance in the library. Vance was quiet and seemed sad. He stuck to Valorie during recess and lunch. He asked me when I was coming home, and I told him I was going to tell Sally to bring me home right away.

---

That night, I begged Sally to take me to my father's house.

"He moved, and I'm not sure where he is," she said, shrugging.

I panicked. I'd had this feeling before. Suddenly, I didn't like living with Sally Doll anymore. I didn't care about the clothes or the popular girls liking me. I didn't care about the ballerina lamp or the beautiful house. I didn't care about all the food in Sally's cabinets. I wanted to be my old self with my brothers and sister. I didn't like Bob, but I loved Valorie, Vance, and Vincent and wanted us to be together again. I wanted to sleep close to Vincent. I realized that fancy stuff didn't make me happy. I was happiest with my brothers and sister. We needed each other. Mom was going to come and get us, and she wouldn't like it if I wasn't taking care of Vincent like I'd promised I would. I was getting more scared with each day.

"I want to go home!" I told Sally. "You have to find my dad. Thank you for everything, but I don't belong to you, I belong to my dad, and my mom is going to come and get us soon."

I was shocked when Sally said I *did* belong to her, and that I should face the fact that my mother was dead—and besides, I was her *collateral.*

I told her she was wrong, and that Bob lied. I didn't want to be her collateral anymore.

She said I had to stay until Bob paid her back the money he owed her.

I didn't understand any of it. All I knew was that my mother wasn't dead, and I wanted to go home.

Now what was I going to do? I needed to find Bob. And how was I going to find my mother?

*God, please send someone to help me. Tell me what to do. Should I run away? Where would I go? Can I ask my teacher? No, because she might call the police, and then I'll never see my brothers and sister again.*

When Sally finally let me go back to school, Valorie and Vance weren't there anymore. I hadn't felt this scared since we left the Philippines.

I prayed my rosary morning and night until I finally came up with a plan. I decided to refuse to eat, shower, or go to school. I lay in bed all day, and late at night, when Sally left for work, I got up and snuck some food and brushed my teeth. I hated not being clean.

For the next couple of nights, I dreamt that Mom came to get us. It was so real that I woke up and looked for her. God was telling me Mom was on her way. I had to get home more than ever.

The next morning, Sally came into my room, crying. She sat on my bed and told me she loved me and asked why I wasn't happy. "I've given you everything you wanted," she said.

All I could say was, "My mother is coming soon, and I need to be with my brothers and sister when she gets here." Then I told her I was sorry. Sally seemed sad, and it was all my fault. I didn't want to make her unhappy, but I didn't have a choice, Mom was coming!

Sally grabbed my shoulders and shook me. "Don't be stupid, Veronica, your mother isn't coming! She is dead; you have to accept that!"

I didn't answer. I just stared at Sally and lay back down on my bed.

Sally thought I was stupid, just like Bob did. Was she a liar too? I could only trust God and my rosary to bring me back to my brothers and sister. I felt I would rather die than be without them.

I didn't eat or go to school that day either. Nothing Sally said could get me out of bed. She started pulling me by my arm, but I pretended like I was dead. I felt dead. Finally, Sally let go of my arm and left me hanging half off the bed. She stomped out and slammed the door hard.

A few seconds later, I heard Sally yelling on the phone, "Come and get her! And I want my money!"

I suddenly realized I wasn't adopted; Bob had *sold* me. That must be what *collateral* meant.

Soon, Bob was at the front door. He was angrier than I'd ever seen him, but I didn't care. Sally told him she'd tried talking sense into me, but nothing had worked. Bob called me an idiot and said I was messing up his life. Now

I had messed up Bob and Sally's lives and made them both unhappy.

I just hung my head and held Vincent's hand.

"Get in the car," Bob snapped.

I didn't take any of my pretty new clothes. I took only what I was wearing: shorts and a T-shirt, my Wednesday underwear, the rosary around my neck, and the black patent leather shoes on my feet.

The four of us hugged and kissed in the backseat of the car. We were together, and nothing was going to separate us again.

⁂

When we got home that night, I told Valorie about the dreams God had sent me. I told her Mom was coming; she was alive!

Valorie looked at me, and I could tell she didn't believe me. "Don't be ridiculous," she said, "Dad's not lying. Why would he lie about Mom dying? Didn't you see how sad he was?" Then she walked away.

We didn't talk about it again. But I knew in my heart that Mom was alive and coming for us. I told Vincent every day that his real mother was on her way.

It was up to me to be patient, pray, and not give up.

## Chapter 14:

# FLEAS

For the next few weeks, our truck was our home. Bob said we had to get out of Dodge fast. We lived in Las Vegas, so I don't know why Bob called it Dodge. We drove through one state after another, and I wondered if we'd ever get to where we were going. Bob drove day and night and said it was an adventure.

Us kids traveled in the back of the beat-up pickup because Bob had sold our Cadillac. He built a house made of wood on the back and called it a camper shell. It reminded me of the seashells in the Philippines that protected the little animals inside. Bob painted it a shiny black, inside and out, and even put in a small window that slid back and forth. Vincent was the only one who could stand up inside the shell; the rest of us were too tall. We slept in sleeping bags, so we didn't have to stop at motels.

We had a red and white cooler in the back with us, filled with ice, Tang, Pabst Blue Ribbon beer, Oscar Meyer bologna, cheese, Skippy peanut butter, and bread. We never had milk because it would go bad. Now we didn't have to stop to eat, either, because we had everything we needed in the cooler. Bob said stopping wasted time. We did stop once in a while to go to the bathroom and wash up while he got gas and cigarettes.

This adventure wasn't fun, and it was taking way too long. I wanted to eat hot food and sleep in a real bed.

When the sun came up after driving all night, I would slide open the little window on the shell to see what state we were in. I always knew where we were by the license plates on the cars speeding by. If most of the plates said New Mexico, then that was the state we were in. The same went for Texas, Louisiana, Mississippi, and Georgia.

On one of our all-night drives, Bob pulled into a truck stop with a gas station. He needed cigarettes, and we needed to go to the bathroom. Valorie and I always got out together and never went into the bathrooms alone, especially at night. All the truck stops were scary and dirty. Once you left the parking lot, it was dark, which made it easy to get lost between all the 18-wheelers. That's what Bob called the big trucks. The 18-wheelers were usually parked near the bathrooms.

Most of the time, Vance and Vincent peed in the bushes, unless they had to go number two. I never let Vincent go into the men's bathroom by himself. I knew in my stomach it wasn't a good idea. Sometimes all four of us went into the same bathroom. We made sure no one was in there first, and then we took turns watching the door. Bob always said there was "safety in numbers," which meant it was better if we stuck together.

This night, the four of us went into the women's bathroom. The women's was always cleaner than the men's. It was pitch black outside. Valorie told us that pitch was like tar—black. So it was like tar outside. Valorie was like Mom; she knew everything.

The bathrooms were behind the Texaco station. I saw two men smoking and watching us as we went into the women's bathroom. I told everyone to hurry. The light inside the bathroom wasn't working, but the one outside was on, so we took turns holding the door open a tiny bit. This let just enough light in to see what we were doing.

Vincent didn't want to go into the stall by himself, so I had Vance hold the door and I went with him into the small, dark, smelly stall. We tried to wash our hands when we were done, but there wasn't any soap, and we had to dry our hands on our T-shirts.

"Let's run!" I said as we headed back to our truck. I couldn't wait to get out of there.

Just as we came to all the 18-wheelers parked next to each other, we saw a dog wandering among the trucks. Vance ran toward the dog, calling, "Here boy, here boy!" The skinny black-and-white dog ran right up to Vance, and we all started petting it. Vincent got excited when the dog licked his face. The dog acted like we were his owners and seemed happy to see us; his tail never stopped wagging.

The black-and-white dog followed us back to our truck. He looked like he needed food, so Vance got some cheese out of the cooler and the dog gobbled it up. Vance wanted to give the dog water, but we didn't have a bowl to put it in. Then he had an idea; he'd let the dog jump into the back of the truck so he could drink the melted ice water at the bottom of the cooler. When we climbed into the truck, the dog jumped right up after us. He was so thirsty and drank for forever.

We loved the dog right away, and he loved us. Vance wanted to find Bob to ask if we could keep him, but Bob was nowhere in sight. He was probably drinking with some new friends. He made friends easily at the truck stops. They shared their beer and cigarettes with him and told stories for hours—stories Bob called Tall Tales, which meant they were made up. Their stories weren't interesting like the ones the Americans told at Lee's Coffee Shop, though.

In back of the truck, we made bologna sandwiches and Tang for ourselves. The dog liked the peanut butter sandwich Vance made for him. We snuggled down into our sleeping bags with the dog right in the middle, a big pile of love.

I don't know what time it was when Bob finally got back, but I woke up when I heard the truck door open. Then I heard the engine start. It must have been very early in the morning, because light was coming in through the little window. It was so cold we could see our breath. We were sandwiched together with the dog snuggled right up against us, helping to keep us warm.

Bob stuck his head in the back of the truck before taking off, I guess to make sure we were all there. It was dark in the back and Bob didn't see the dog—not until it growled at him.

"What the hell is that damn dog doing in this truck?" he yelled.

Now the dog was barking. I think he was trying to protect us. Bob reached in and tried to grab him, but he growled and showed his teeth. We all started yelling to please not hurt the dog, and Bob yelled, "Get that dirty damn dog out of the truck this instant!"

Bob smelled like beer, and we knew not to make him mad when he smelled like beer. We all started crying and begging him to let us keep the dog. Vance had his arms around the dog's neck. Valorie said the dog had chased away a man who was trying to steal the truck. Vance said he was a good watchdog because he barked whenever anyone came near us. I told Bob about the two men near the bathroom and how we needed the dog to protect us. I didn't know why Valorie lied about it chasing a man away, but it seemed to work; Bob's face started to look a little less angry.

"That dog is probably flea bitten!" he said.

Fleas, our beloved dog

I didn't know how he could possibly know if the dog had been bitten by fleas, but I didn't care if we all did. We promised Bob we'd wash the dog and take care of him. He would be our responsibility.

Bob gave up. He slammed the door at the back of the truck and walked away.

Once we felt the truck starting to move, we all clapped quietly. We named our new dog Fleas.

Fleas was the best dog ever. From that moment on, we took him with us into the bathrooms at the truck stops as our bodyguard. We weren't afraid to go anywhere if we had Fleas with us. I don't know how he always knew who was nice and who wasn't, but he did.

Fleas traveled in the back of the truck all through Texas. He was one of us now.

## Chapter 15:

# BLACK PATENT LEATHER SHOES

In 1961, I was ten years old and in the fourth grade. I missed a lot of school that year, so I was still in the fourth grade when we arrived at our new home in Florence, Texas.

We drove up a dirt road to an old farmhouse just outside Florence.

"This is the end of the road," Bob said, which meant we could finally get out of the truck and stay out. It was so hot in the back! We took turns putting our heads out the window, but it wasn't much help. Fleas liked it best. I think it cooled him off too.

Our new house was dusty, dirty, and had broken windows. There was no running water or inside bathroom. Bob said it was all he could afford, because having four children and no job left him little choice on where we could live. I didn't care; anything was better than living in the truck.

I liked the idea of living on a farm; it sounded exciting. Tall grass surrounded the house, along with plenty of trees.

I saw a real adventure, not a broken-down house, and it was much better than anything we'd lived in for a while. This was going to be much more fun than our driving adventure.

There was a real covered wagon out front, next to the dirt road. Bob said the wagon was a hundred years old. I tried to imagine who'd ridden in that wagon a hundred years ago and was sure it was bumpier than our truck. It had four giant wooden wheels, two benches inside, and was half-covered with torn material. It was the perfect playhouse.

Across the dirt road from the covered wagon was a stream. A tall, skinny man in overalls greeted us when we arrived. He told us that the stream had tadpoles in it and the water was crystal clear and ice cold and if we followed it, it became a much bigger stream with live fish in it. That sounded like a perfect place to be on a hot dusty day.

Bob walked onto the front porch of the farmhouse with the tall skinny man. They were both smoking, and by the looks on their faces, they were talking about something serious.

Since they were busy talking, the four of us took off exploring. We didn't ask permission; we just ran in all directions. I helped Vincent into the wagon and told him to stay there until I came to get him. He looked cute sitting in the shade of the material hanging in the wagon. Valorie and Vance dashed across the dirt road to the tadpole stream, Fleas running after them. I ran to the open field alongside the farmhouse, hoping to see cows or horses.

I had never seen a place like this before. We'd always lived in places with lots of cars and people—where all the buildings were close together. This place was paradise! I was wearing my only dress and my black patent leather shoes. I went running through the field, looking for animals, but didn't see any cows or horses. I was so disappointed.

I heard Vance yelling for me. "Come see all the little fish," he cried.

I ran back toward the farmhouse. It was getting pretty hot anyway, and I needed to check on Vincent. As I was running back, I saw a small black-and-white cat. It wasn't the cow or horse I was hoping to see, but at least it was an animal. I loved animals, especially kittens. I wanted to get that cat to show Vance, so I took off after it.

Suddenly, the cat ran down a hole in the ground. I was in luck, because now I had it cornered. I got down on my knees and stuck my hand into the hole. I couldn't feel anything, so I lay on my stomach and tried to reach a little further. I knew I was going to get in trouble for getting my dress dirty, but I didn't care because I was so close to my prize.

By lying on my stomach, I was able to stretch my arm deep into the hole. I felt the cat, grabbed it, and pulled it out by its tail. I held it way out in front of me because it was trying to bite me. I ran toward the farmhouse, where Bob and the tall skinny man were, and yelled, "Look what I found!" I was so excited. Vance and Valorie came running.

All of a sudden, I smelled something awful. It made me want to throw up, and I couldn't breathe.

Bob turned, looked at me, and began yelling, "Drop it!" He ran toward me and the tall, skinny man grabbed a shovel that was leaning against the farmhouse.

I dropped the cat. Before it could run away, the tall, skinny man hit it with the shovel. The cat looked dead and was bleeding from its head. I was afraid he was going to hit me next. I wanted to cry, but my lungs were burning. I thought I was going to faint.

Bob grabbed my arm and jerked me toward the house. The tall, skinny man went into the house and filled a big washbasin from the pump on the kitchen sink. I'd never seen water come out that way.

"Take off all your clothes," Bob commanded.

Everyone was standing around, staring at me. Vincent looked frightened.

I was confused but knew to obey orders. I took off my dress and shoes and stood there, shivering, in just my underwear. I wasn't cold; I was waiting for something bad to happen to me. I didn't understand why I was being punished. *I* didn't kill the cat.

"It would be best if we buried her clothes," the tall, skinny man said.

What was going on? All I could do was stand there and cry. No one was coming to help me.

Bob told Valorie and Vance to get the shovel and dig a deep hole outside in the grassy area. The tall skinny man picked up all my clothes—including my black patent leather shoes—and headed out of the house. He pushed the torn screen door open so hard it made a loud bang. I jumped and started to cry louder. My only dress and my favorite shoes were going into a hole in the ground. Why? Why was this happening?

Bob started to scrub me hard with soap that smelled like Elmer's glue. The water was icy cold. After scrubbing me from head to toe, he told Vance to get the Old Spice out of his bag. I loved the smell, but it stung my raw skin as Bob poured it over me.

"You're lucky that skunk didn't bite her," the tall, skinny man said to Bob. "They all have rabies, you know."

I couldn't believe I'd caught a skunk. It hadn't looked anything like Pepé Le Pew on the cartoons. And I didn't know what rabies was, but it couldn't be good.

Bob started calling me Stinky that day. He thought he was being funny. Valorie chimed in and called me Stinky too. I didn't care. It was only a word. All I cared about were my black patent leather shoes. How was I going to get another pair?

Bob and the tall, skinny man shook hands and we unloaded our truck. The farmhouse was our new home.

---

For the next several days, we cleaned and swept, then swept some more. The pump in the kitchen was fun. You had to push down on this long handle to make water come out. If you stopped pushing on the handle the water would stop.

The bathroom wasn't fun. It was a small wooden shed out back that Bob called an "outhouse," because you had to leave the house to use it. Now *that* was stinky! To make matters worse, for the next several days the only toilet paper was an old Sears and Roebuck's catalog lying on the outhouse floor.

A few weeks into our stay, we were dressed and sitting in the old wagon out front, waiting for the school bus. I didn't have my only dress anymore, so I wore a pair of faded blue pedal pushers I'd gotten at the Goodwill. Thank goodness for my white blouse. I wore it with everything.

Bob had taken Vincent to a house up the road where two old ladies lived. They would watch him until I got home.

The school bus arrived, and we got on. The kids on the bus didn't know what to make of us. I heard someone say, "They look like poor kids."

If I'd had my black patent leather shoes on, they wouldn't have said that.

The bus stopped several more times to pick up kids from the farms in the area, and none of those farms looked like ours. They were all big, with white fences and beautiful horses running around. The kids on the bus were laughing and goofing around. I sat next to Vance. Valorie sat next to a blond girl. I heard Valorie trying to make friends with her by telling her about the skunk I caught. The girl started laughing and said out loud, "You mean, she didn't know the difference between a cat and a skunk? How dumb is she?"

Everyone on the bus was laughing, and that was just the beginning. By the next day, the whole school knew the skunk story. I wasn't going to be happy at Brown Stone Elementary no. 39.

I wondered if I could ask God for two things: Mom and another pair of black patent leather shoes.

Chapter 16:

# AFRAID OF THE DARK

I'd never held a gun before, but today I would, whether I wanted to or not. After a few beers, Bob announced that it was time we all learned how to shoot.

"It's time to fix dinner," I complained. "It will be dark soon."

"We don't need a lot of light," he said. "And getting dinner is exactly what we're going to do; we're going to hunt for our dinner."

What? We all just looked at each other. I was sure Bob had something in mind, something I wasn't going to like. Or maybe he was kidding; you never knew with Bob.

He loaded us up in our pick-up truck and off we went. Did he really want us to shoot a living animal? I suggested we go to the end of the stream and catch some fish.

"No," he said, "it's time you learned to live off the land."

I wasn't sure what that meant. When Bob was drinking, you never knew what he was talking about until it happened or until it was too late.

Bob always carried a shotgun and a rifle behind the seat of our truck. Everyone in Texas did. Before we left the house, he said it would be exciting to ride around in the back of the truck. Sometimes it was, but I had a feeling in my stomach that this wasn't one of those times.

I'd been glad when Bob took the camper shell off the truck; it was more fun riding into town without it. Fleas loved it most of all. When he put his paws on the side of the truck and leaned out, the wind would blow in his face so hard that he looked like he was smiling.

Tonight, though, I didn't think being tossed around in the back of the truck was a good idea. Shooting guns when Bob was drinking wasn't a good idea, either. I felt the best place for us to be was in our room.

Once, Bob had made Valorie drive the truck home after he'd drunk a lot of beer. She'd done a pretty good job getting us home for being only eleven. Another time, he drank so much beer, he forgot us at a bar. These were the things Bob did when he drank. It was never good, and tonight wouldn't be any different.

We drove out to the open field behind the farmhouse, with Bob driving back and forth a little too fast. The ride in the bed of the truck was exciting but scary at the same time as we fell from side to side. Once, it felt like we were going to turn over. I was glad I'd made Vincent ride up front with Valorie.

It was starting to get dark, so I knocked on the back window. Bob stopped the truck and slid open the window.

"I want to go home," I said. "I'm sure we have some food left over from our last trip to the army base." We got free food there every month.

He ignored me, as usual, then asked, "Who wants to learn how to shoot?"

Vance raised his hand and said, "Me, me!"

Bob climbed into the back of the truck and handed Vance the shotgun. Vance said it was too heavy. Bob told him not to be a sissy, then showed him how to hold the gun up against his shoulder. Vance tried to hold the gun and do exactly what Bob told him to do. I felt sorry for him; he just wanted to pull the trigger so he could put down the heavy gun.

"Do you see that tree over there?" Bob said.

Vance was scared, and I don't think he saw what Bob wanted him to see, but he answered "yes" anyway.

"Then pull the damn trigger."

As soon as Vance did, he ended up on the floor of the truck and started to cry.

Now Bob was really mad, yelling and calling Vance a sissy girl.

I could see he was going to make Vance do it again, so I quickly picked up the gun and said, "I want to shoot next."

Bob leaned me up against the back window of the truck. He then took a piece of rope, tied it around my waist, and attached the ends to hooks on the side of the truck. I could hardly breathe.

"Now you won't fall on your butt," he said.

I didn't like this at all and felt forced to do something bad.

I should have said "no," but I never said "no." I hadn't said "no" when Bob took us from the coffee shop or "no" to the nuns when he said we were adopted or "no" to the hairdresser when I didn't like my blond hair, but worst of all I hadn't said "no" when they buried my black patent leather shoes. I was afraid to say no to Bob. I didn't want him to get angry at me and start yelling.

Bob got back in the truck and started to drive. I was frozen with fear. He yelled out the window, "Shoot!"

I didn't aim at anything; I just closed my eyes and pulled the trigger. Instantly I felt pain in my shoulder where the gun was, but I didn't fall backwards because the rope worked. Vance was still crying quietly in the corner behind me.

It was dark now, and Bob stopped again. We were in the middle of the back pasture, in a clearing with no trees. He told me he was going to shine the headlights into a rabbit's eyes. There were hundreds of rabbits. When the rabbit stopped, I was to shoot it. He told me the headlights would blind the rabbits, and they would freeze.

*A rabbit was going to be our dinne*r? I couldn't believe it.

Bob started to drive again. I heard Valorie yell from up front, "There, there! It's a rabbit!"

The poor rabbit stopped and stared into the headlights of the truck, just like Bob said it would. I didn't even try to shoot in the rabbit's direction, though I don't think I could have hit it if I had. It got away, "Thank you God," I said under my breath.

Bob continued to drive. Then he stopped suddenly, jumped out of the truck with his rifle, and shot a rabbit. A few minutes later, he shot a second one. Then we headed home.

---

Valorie was the cook in the family, so back at the house, Bob showed her how to skin a rabbit. I couldn't even watch. The bunnies ended up on our barbecue. I realized then why we had to shoot those rabbits: we were poor and needed food.

Once dinner was ready, I couldn't eat it. After everyone was done picking at the rabbit, Bob told Vance to stay outside. Fleas was tied up in front of the house, and he started barking, he wanted to go to Vance. Fleas loved all of us, but he was really Vance's dog.

"Why does Vance have to stay outside?" I asked. I had a bad feeling in my stomach.

"Vance is a sissy, and he needs to learn to be a man," Bob said. "The rest of you, stay in the house." He stomped outside.

I looked out the window and heard Bob tell Vance to pick between a rifle and a flashlight. I didn't understand what was going on. Vance was afraid of the dark—had been since we lived at St. Clara's. He never closed the door at night, and there always had to be light, even if it was just a little.

It was pitch black out now.

Vance chose the flashlight.

"Get back in the truck," Bob said.

Fleas started barking like crazy, trying to get free. The truck drove off into the night.

Bob and Vance were gone for a long time.

When I heard the truck coming back, I ran outside. Fleas started barking again. Bob got out of the truck, but Vance wasn't with him.

"Where's Vance?" I yelled louder than I wanted to.

"I needed to teach Vance a lesson," Bob said.

*Where was he?* I was so worried about him. I wanted to untie Fleas because I knew he would find him.

Bob must have read my mind because he turned to me and said, "Don't try and untie that damn dog or you will be next."

*Next for what?* I thought.

I didn't sleep that night.

⁂

Early the next morning, when it was still dark, I got dressed quietly. Everyone else was asleep. I untied Fleas and told him to come with me. I told him not to bark, and he seemed to understand.

The sun wasn't up yet but there was just enough light for Fleas and me to see. I told Fleas to find Vance; he took off running. It was cold but peaceful: the birds were chirping back and forth to each other, and it smelled fresh and clean as I ran after Fleas.

"Slow down!" I called softly. "Wait for me!"

He listened, and we walked together across the field. Where was my brother?

We were now far enough away from the farmhouse for me to start calling Vance's name. I made sure not to call out too loud. I didn't want Bob to hear me. He'd had a lot of beer the night before, so I was pretty sure he'd sleep for a few more hours.

Suddenly, Fleas started running again, and I ran after him.

I started calling louder now: "Vance! Vancee! Vanceeeee!"

Fleas found Vance first. As I ran toward a patch of trees, I heard Vance crying and saying, "I'm here. Over here!"

There he was: curled up under a big tree, clutching his flashlight, wrapped in the old army blanket we kept in the back of the truck, trembling with fear and cold. He grabbed me, and we hugged. Then he put an arm around Fleas's neck. Fleas wouldn't stop licking Vance's face.

"What happened?" I asked him.

"Dad said I could protect myself with a gun like a man or hold on to the flashlight like a sissy," Vance said. He was more afraid of the dark than being eaten by wild animals, so he picked the flashlight.

Bob told him there were wolves. I was sure Vance had

thought he wasn't going to make it through the night.

"There are no wolves around here," I told him. "Only bunnies, raccoons, skunks, and armadillos." Then I told him what I always told Vincent: "Everything is going to be alright."

We were both hungry. Vance took my hand, and we headed home with Fleas close to his side.

Vance never slept with a light on again.

Afraid of the dark, downtown Florence

## Chapter 17:

# THE PINK LUNCH CARD

I asked Bob if we could go into town. I wanted to get something from Foodland. But he kept saying, "Later."

Why couldn't he take me now? He wasn't doing anything but lying on the couch smoking and drinking beer.

"We only have two beers left," I said trying to convince him, "we should go get some more. And I just want to get one other thing too." It was important we leave soon, because Bob was usually drunk by 3:00 p.m. on Sundays, so if I waited until then he'd never take me.

"What's the rush?" Bob said. "I'll get what we need tomorrow, and we still have Spam and rice for dinner."

"I need to buy some Barbara Ann Bread," I said. "I want to make a sandwich for school tomorrow."

"Use your pink lunch card," he said.

I begged him, but he said we didn't need bread. If only he knew how badly I needed *that* bread.

Barbara Ann Bread had a picture of a beautiful little girl with golden blond hair on the package. She had blue eyes, a matching blue bow in her hair, and a blue dress with a perfect white Peter Pan collar. Barbara Ann was perfect, perfect, perfect. I wished I could be her. I hated using my pink lunch card.

I wanted to make my favorite sandwich: mayonnaise sprinkled with sugar between two pieces of Barbara Ann's soft, white bread. When other kids brought their lunches to school, they always had Oscar Meyer bologna or peanut butter and jelly between two pieces of Barbara Ann's bread. I liked sugar and mayonnaise better and couldn't think of anything more delicious for lunch.

When I had to use my pink lunch card, I'd try to be the last kid in line. I would fold my pink lunch card up really small, hiding it in the palm of my hand. I didn't know why they had to make those pink lunch cards so big. By the end of the week my lunch card always looked like it had been through a washing machine. My hand would sweat when I squeezed my lunch card tight, hoping no one would see even a little piece of it.

Now that Bob wasn't going to take me into town, I had two choices: I could skip lunch, or use my pink lunch card. Skipping lunch was always risky because I never knew if there would be any food when I got home. I checked the cabinets to see what we had left in the food department. After looking all through the kitchen, I realized I'd have to use my pink lunch card. We weren't going to the base to get more food for at least a week.

Valorie could always make something out of nothing. Once she took some dried beans and boiled them. She cut up a can of Spam with a tomato and onion the old ladies up the road had given us and boiled everything for a long time—and it was delicious. She said it was like the story of the old man who made nail soup. I loved that story.

The Fort Hood army base was not too far from where we lived in Florence. Every month, we piled into our truck for the trip to the base, where soldiers would give us a big box of free food. Bob said it was because he used to be in the army. The soldiers had lots of boxes already packed, and there was one for each family. Inside was powered milk, Velveeta cheese, sugar, beans, rice, coffee, and Spam—lots of Spam. Sometimes the soldiers gave us kids Hersey chocolate bars. We'd cross our fingers all the way to the base, hoping for chocolate.

I wished the base would give us Barbara Ann Bread, but everything they gave us didn't spoil no matter how long we had it. The food was non-perishable. That's what it said on the big box. When we left the base, Bob would take us to the market to get eggs, cinnamon rolls, milk, and, if we were lucky, apples. Bob paid with fake paper money he called stamps. The only time Bob used real money was when he was buying beer or cigarettes. The store wouldn't take the stamps for those things. I bet they knew beer wasn't good for you and cigarettes smelled.

Because we were low on food, I had to use my pink lunch card. This wouldn't be a good week to skip lunch, at least not until our next trip to the base. At least I didn't have to worry about Vincent eating; the two old ladies on the farm up the road, Louise and Clair, took care of him when we were in school, and they always fed him. They were real sisters, like Valorie and me, not sisters like the nuns. They said they were "old maids." I wondered if they used to be maids like Soling, and I wondered how old Soling was now. Clair said an old maid was what you called a lady who never got married. I thought Soling must be an old maid too.

The sisters baked and cooked really good food for Vincent at their house. I liked walking up the dusty dirt road to pick him up when I got off the school bus. When I arrived, the old ladies always had a treat for me: oatmeal cookies with fresh milk or lemonade or the best egg salad sandwich in town. They also gave me tomatoes and onions from their garden to bring home. Valorie told me not to forget to bring the vegetables if they offered them, but I knew better than to tell the sisters I was hungry.

The best part of picking up Vincent was watching TV. The TV they had was small, so you had to sit really close. I loved watching *The Andy Griffith Show* and *Leave It to Beaver*. If Bob wasn't home, Vincent and I would spend a little extra time with Louise and Clair, watching *What's My Line?* I wished I belonged to one of those TV families.

I never stayed too long at their house, because if I did, they would ask how our father was and if he was home. I always said, "He's fine and yes, he's probably home now so I better get going before he gets worried." I was never to tell anyone he wasn't home.

---

On Monday, when the lunch bell rang, everyone rushed to the cafeteria. It smelled so good that my stomach was growling. There was spaghetti with meatballs, mashed potatoes with gravy, perfectly sliced green beans, hamburger patties, green Jell-O, rice pudding, and corn bread. You had a choice of plain milk or chocolate milk, too. I was starving.

I got in line and held my head up like I belonged there. I picked up my brown tray, my napkin, a silver fork, and a silver spoon. I put my tray on the metal counter, pushing it slowly along behind a girl with pretty blond hair just like

Barbara Ann's. She was talking with her friends, and I heard her say, "This food stinks."

How could she say that? The food smelled wonderful.

The blond girl hardly took anything. I took one of everything. She glanced back at me, then down to my full tray. I kept holding my head up. When she got to the cash register, she opened her shiny white purse and pulled out a whole dollar. I waited until she started to walk away. I pretended I was looking for something in my pocket. I was terrified she'd see that I had a pink lunch card.

The boy behind me was too busy goofing off to pay attention to what I had wadded up in my hand. I quickly handed the lady at the register my pink card; she reminded me of the black lady on the Aunt Jemima syrup bottle, especially when she smiled and showed her big white teeth. She was always very friendly, smiling at me when she punched my pink lunch card. But today, to my horror, she said a little too loudly, "Go on, sugar, your food is free."

I felt hot. I held my breath. I was praying the girl in front of me hadn't hear what Aunt Jemima had said. I mumbled under my breath, "Please don't turn around." I rushed off with my tray full of one of everything.

The girl who'd been in front of me whispered something to her friend, and they both laughed. I was sure they were laughing at me. Only poor kids got pink lunch cards.

Pink was never going to be my favorite color.

## Chapter 18:

# THE PEP RALLY

Valorie, Vance, and I couldn't wait to get off the school bus. It was hot, and they wanted to go down to the tadpole stream, but I ran ahead of them as fast as I could, right into the house. The torn screen door slammed behind me.

At school, things had been going pretty well these past couple of months, and now I had a chance to make things even better. I was calling for Bob as I searched the two bedrooms, kitchen, and back porch. Valorie and Vance came in a few seconds behind me, took off their shoes, and tried to talk me into going with them to the tadpole stream. Any other day, they wouldn't even have had to ask; the tadpole stream was our favorite place. The trees hung down over the water, making lots of shade; there were always plenty of dragonflies to catch; and the water was clean, cold, and full of tadpoles. Today, though, I told them to go without me.

I was so excited! I had to find Bob. His truck was parked out front, next to the old covered wagon, but where was he? He had to take me into town.

I searched the back pasture and the old barn. He was nowhere to be found. No big surprise; I figured he must have gone to the cowboy bar in town with some of his soldier friends from Fort Hood.

I wondered if I should wait for him or run up the road to the sisters' house and ask them for a ride into town. We could take Vincent with us. Maybe I could ride Snow to the sisters' house.

Snow was an old white mare given to us for nothing. A man had given us her saddle and everything. It was easy to climb onto her using the back-porch steps. We loved riding her around the property. She never went fast; she'd gallop a little sometimes, but mostly she walked. Lots of times, she would just stop when she got tired, and then you had to slide off and pull her by the reins all the way home.

Once, I was riding Snow around the property when she came to a complete stop. I started to slide off, but then I noticed cactus on both sides. Snow had stopped in a cactus patch. I was barefoot, so I started to gently kick her, like I'd seen other people do when they wanted their horse to go. I had never kicked Snow before and didn't know why kicking made a horse go—it seemed to me it would only make a horse mad—but it seemed worth a try. But it didn't work.

I tried pleading with her. I scooted my butt back and forth in the saddle. No luck. I would have to sit and wait until someone saw me, or until Snow decided to head home.

Finally, she started to move. I wore shoes whenever I rode her from then on.

I decided against riding Snow when I remembered the saddle; I couldn't put it on her by myself. And I didn't want to take the chance of her stopping, anyway. So I ran up the dusty road as fast as I could.

It was mostly uphill. The sweat was running down my face and into my eyes. My white blouse was soaked by the time I reached the sisters' house. I knocked even though they told me I never had to; I could just come in. Mom taught me to always knock because it was polite.

Clair was watching TV and Louise was in the kitchen with Vincent, who heard me knocking and came running. He always hugged me like he hadn't seen me for a long time. He probably didn't want to lose me like we'd lost Mom.

I was out of breath, and my mouth was so dry I could hardly talk. Louise came out of the kitchen with an ice-cold glass of lemonade. I drank it down without taking a breath and thanked her.

"Do you own a sewing machine?" I asked once I could talk again.

"Yes," Louise said. "Do you want to learn to sew?"

"Yes," I said, "but not today. Could you please drive me into town? It's very important. I need to get some orange material to make a skirt—not much, just enough to go around my waist." I begged them to help me. "It doesn't have to be perfect," I said. "We can pin it in the back with a few safety pins."

If I had an orange skirt, then all I needed was my white blouse—which wasn't really white anymore, but it was close enough. I'd take it off and wash it as soon as I got home. The top button was missing, but I had a pin for that too.

The sisters wanted to know how soon I needed the skirt, and I explained that it was for the day after tomorrow.

"Oh, we can whip that up, no problem," Louise said.

I was so relieved.

I was going to be in the Pep Rally! The third, fourth, and fifth grade girls were going to cheer for our football team. To be in the Pep Rally, you had to wear a white blouse and an orange skirt and sit in a special section of the bleachers. Our job was to cheer for our team by yelling as loud as we could. I was feeling special. I was feeling normal.

The sisters explained that they couldn't drive me into town because their car was in the shop, but not to worry because I had two days, and as soon as my father got home, they were sure he would take me into town. They told me I only needed one yard, and it would be easy. I felt better when they said that. They even had a zipper for my skirt, which meant I wouldn't have to use safety pins. I thanked and hugged them both, and said I'd be back soon with the yard of material.

Vincent and I walked home quickly. We held hands and swung our arms back and forth. Vincent was singing, "Lou, lou, skip to my lou; skip to my lou my darling!" I wondered who'd taught him that song. I sang along with him and smiled all the way home.

---

When Bob finally came home that evening, he was drunk, and it was too late to go into town anyway, so there was no use talking to him that night. I'd have to wait and ask him about getting my yard of orange material in the morning. He listened better when he hadn't been drinking.

The sisters had already measured my waist and the length for my skirt. They said it would only take a couple of hours to make. I was excited just thinking about my orange skirt.

I knew Bob didn't have much money, but Louise said it wouldn't cost much. They said one yard of material would be about fifty cents at Mr. Thompson's general store, and I knew Bob could afford that! He smoked and drank beer every day and that had to cost almost a dollar. He had to have an extra fifty cents for my skirt.

⁂

The next morning, I told Bob all about the Pep Rally. I told him how badly I needed to buy some orange material to make my skirt. He seemed interested and even asked if parents could go.

I told him yes.

I told him I wanted him to go.

I told him he could watch me cheer in my orange skirt and white blouse.

I told him the other girls were starting to be nice to me.

I told him no one mentioned the skunk anymore.

I told him the old ladies said they'd make my skirt and I only needed a yard.

I told him it would cost less than a dollar.

I was talking so fast I hardly took a breath. Bob smiled and promised to take me to town as soon as I got home from school. He said he'd buy the material and take me up to the sisters' house. I thanked him and gave him a big hug and kiss. I didn't usually kiss Bob, but I felt like it that morning. I was so happy.

That afternoon, I got off the bus and ran into the house. Bob wasn't home yet, but I was sure he'd be home any second. He'd promised. While I was waiting, I cleaned up the house. I swept the front porch and did all the dishes. I told Valorie to make Spam and rice while I went to get Vincent. Bob loved Valorie's rice and fried Spam.

I ran up the road as fast as I could. When I got to the sisters' house, I told them I'd be back shortly with the material. They said they'd thread the sewing machine and have everything ready. I told Vincent I'd race him home so he'd run fast and we'd get there quicker. I always let him win.

I waited. I waited until dark for Bob to come home. When he finally came home, it was too late. All the stores had closed, and the sisters were sleeping for sure.

I pretended to be asleep when he looked in our room. Why had I believed him? I wished I hadn't kissed him.

I didn't go to school the day of the Pep Rally.

I stayed home sick.

## Chapter 19:

# I HAVE A JOB!

Pushing the big broom around was harder than I thought it would be. A few weeks earlier, I'd asked Mr. Jackson if he needed help. Mr. Jackson was the school janitor who swept every classroom, every afternoon, after every kid had left. He said he had been pushing a broom for over forty years. I could hardly believe he had lived in this small town for that long.

I told Mr. Jackson I needed the job so I could save money for a new pair of black patent leather shoes. He looked at me for a minute then said, "Actually, I could use a little help. I'm not as fast as I use to be." I thanked Mr. Jackson and told him he wouldn't regret hiring me. I was a hard worker and wouldn't let him down. The school bus didn't leave until 3:45 p.m. every day, so that gave me an hour to work for him.

I met Mr. Jackson in the cafeteria after school the next day. First, I collected the small trash cans in every classroom.

There were only twelve classrooms at my school, one for each grade. I dumped the small trash cans into a very large metal trash can on Mr. Jackson's cart. I was surprised how much good stuff got thrown away. I found perfectly good crayons and half-eaten candy bars, and once I even found a pair of pink barrettes with small white birds on them. They looked brand-new. I had never owned barrettes because they cost money; I used rubber bands to keep my hair out of my face. I gave the barrettes to Mr. Jackson, because I was sure someone had dropped them in the trash by accident. He told me to keep them. They weren't mine, so I put them on the teacher's desk. I didn't like pink anyway.

Mr. Jackson's cart had all kinds of cleaning things hanging off of it. There were brushes, brooms, dustpans, bottles of cleaning fluid, rags, and, on the back of the cart, the big trash can. His cart was so heavy, Mr. Jackson had to lean forward to make it move. I was thinking how hard it must be to push a big cart like his for forty years.

After a few weeks of emptying trash cans, Mr. Jackson showed me how to push his big broom. He told me I was smart, and I shouldn't be a broom pusher all my life like him. It made me feel special when he said I was smart.

Mr. Jackson was a tall, thin, black man who wore the same blue overalls every day. He whistled while he pushed his big broom and said hello to every person that passed us by. The teachers said hello back but none of the students did. That wasn't polite, but Mr. Jackson didn't seem to mind. He was always in a good mood. He gave me a dime at the end of each cleaning day.

I had a job! I never wanted to miss school because I never wanted to miss work. I was so excited and could feel my black patent shoes on my feet already.

I kept my dimes in my *secret box*, a small green metal box I'd found in the old barn out back when Vance and I went exploring one day. Bob told us not to go in there because of black widow spiders, rattlesnakes, and boards with nails sticking out of them. We went anyway.

There were all kinds of interesting things in the barn. I didn't know what most of the stuff was for. Everything looked really old. The little green box was on a shelf and had rusty nails in it. I didn't think anyone would want it, so I emptied out the rusty nails and kept it. When I got the box home, I washed it out and decided it would make a good place to keep all my special things, like the picture of my mother that Grandma Phyllis had given me, my pearl necklace that the lady with the baby had given me, my rosary, a lucky Philippine penny called a centavo, and a couple of Vincent's baby teeth. I put everything I wanted to keep safe in my little green box; it was my secret hiding place.

I started putting my dimes in my secret box. With so many dimes, I knew I had to find a good hiding place. I decided to hide it near the tree where Vance had spent the night the night Bob got mad and called him a sissy. I knew I'd never forget that place or that night.

The tree was much bigger than any other tree around, so it was easy to find. I dug a hole deep enough for the box. I took one of Bob's handkerchiefs to line the hole. He had three of them, so I figured he wouldn't notice if one was missing. I set my box into the hole but didn't cover it with dirt. Instead, I put a large rock over the top. No one would know it was there but me.

I worked every day and loved it. Some of the kids made fun of me, but I didn't care because it was the only way I was going to get my special shoes. I told Mr. Jackson I was poor

My secret box

and didn't have many friends. No one seemed to like poor kids. Mr. Jackson said it was the same for him, not because he was poor but because he was a Negro. I supposed it wasn't good to be poor or a Negro, and Mr. Jackson was both. But I liked him. He was my friend and the only person I could really talk to.

My brothers, sister, and I looked a little different than most of the kids in my school. I thought I didn't have many friends because we were poor, but Mr. Jackson said some people in the town were prejudiced. He told me that when people were from another county or spoke another language, people tended not to like them, especially if they weren't Christian.

"Why wouldn't they like you just because you're from somewhere else or go to a different church?" I asked.

"That's a good question," Mr. Jackson answered, and continued to push his broom. He said his grandfather had been a slave, and that was why people were prejudiced toward him. I told him our grandfather had been a warrior in the Philippines and people still didn't like us much. Then I stopped talking, because now I had to think of a way to make people like me. It was much harder to make friends in America. It had been so easy in the Philippines.

Sometimes I'd miss the school bus because there was so much trash to collect. When that happened, I got a ride home from Mrs. Valentine, the vice principal. She seemed to like me. She stayed later than the other teachers, doing work in her office. Mrs. Valentine said she passed right by the road I lived on and didn't mind dropping me off. I think she was my friend too.

I had almost fifty dimes when Vincent got sick. One late afternoon, when Mrs. Valentine dropped me off, I found

Vincent home alone. He was in bed, coughing hard. Why wasn't Bob home? The old ladies up the road hadn't been able to watch Vincent for a few days because they were out of town, and Bob had told me he was going to stay home with him so I could go to school.

I asked Vincent where everyone was, but he didn't know. He looked sad and tired. I was sure Valorie and Vance had gone straight to the tadpole stream after school. When Bob wasn't home, that was always the first place they headed to when they got off the bus.

Bob didn't come home that night. Vincent was coughing so much that none of us could sleep. He felt hot when I touched any part of his little body. He wouldn't eat but was thirsty and drank all the Tang I gave him. He looked so unhappy; I slept close to him all night.

---

Early the next morning, before anyone was awake, I went to my hiding place and took out my secret box. I put all my dimes in an old sock and tied the top tight, then I stuffed the sock into the pocket of my jacket.

I told Vincent to stay in bed until I got home. I made him more Tang and a Spam sandwich before I left.

I wore my jacket to school that day, even though it was hot outside. I didn't want anyone to see my money.

After I was done helping Mr. Jackson, I asked Mrs. Valentine if she could drive me home. She said yes and asked why I wasn't taking the school bus; it hadn't left yet.

"I need to stop at the drug store to buy some cough medicine for my brother," I said.

She frowned. "Why isn't your father getting the medicine?"

"He gave me the money to get it in case he has to work late," I said quickly.

I never knew if I was telling the truth anymore. Lying about our life had become natural. I had to lie. I had to make sure we stayed together.

We stopped at the drug store, and I ran in. I didn't know why it was called a drug store, since Mr. Mason sold everything. I thought it should be called an everything store.

I wanted to look at the comic books but didn't want to keep Mrs. Valentine waiting. I glanced at one with my name on it: *Archie and Veronica*. I thought I'd like to read that one to Vincent.

I bought Vicks cough syrup, Bayer baby aspirin, and Vicks VapoRub. I'd seen all these things on TV at the sisters' house, and the children in the commercials seemed to get well fast. In those commercials, the kids had nice bedrooms and mothers who tucked them into bed with hugs and kisses. I was sure having a mother was the best medicine of all, because moms made everything better. I wanted our mother to come and make everything better. She had to come, because I didn't know how to make things better anymore. Sometimes I'd dream that Mom was never coming, and I'd wake up crying. The only thing that made me feel good was praying my rosary. I'd beg God not to forget about us. I couldn't give up. I had to keep remembering what Mom said: "Be patient, God will hear you."

The total came to almost five dollars, most of my fifty dimes.

"Do I have enough left for a comic book and some Pixy Stix, Mr. Mason?" I asked.

"Yes," he said, without even looking at how much change I had. He put the Pixy Stix in the bag, along with

Vincent's medicine. "You just grab the comic book on your way out," he said.

He was a nice man. I thanked Mr. Mason and ran out the door.

⁂

When we reached our house, Mrs. Valentine seemed worried and wanted to come in and check on Vincent. I told her he wasn't that sick, and my father would be home any minute. She gave me her phone number and said to call her if I needed anything. I said I would.

That was a lie too. We didn't have a phone.

I gave Vincent the cough medicine and rubbed his chest with the Vicks VapoRub, the way I'd seen it done on TV. Then I read him the comic book with my name on it while he sucked on his Pixy Stix. Before he fell asleep, I put a baby aspirin in his mouth. He liked it.

By morning, Vincent wasn't hot anymore, and he hadn't coughed all night. I stayed home with him the next day and hoped I wouldn't lose my job.

My black patent leather shoes would just have to wait.

## Chapter 20:

# ANNA MAY

Bob kicked open the torn screen door, a big box in his arms. He told us to look through it, pick out an outfit, and dress up, because we were going to Anna May's house for dinner.

The box was a donation from one of the churches in town. It seemed wherever we went, people gave us stuff. I knew it was because we were poor.

Anna May was a lady Bob had been visiting a lot. She owned the biggest dairy farm in Florence, and everyone knew her. When we went into town to pick up supplies or to the post office, every single person said hello to her. Men in cowboy hats would tip them and nod their heads. I'm not sure why they did that, but it reminded me of bowing my head when I entered a church in the Philippines. Anna May was very popular.

I wished I was popular.

Anna May was a widow, and she was much older and not as pretty as the other ladies Bob had liked. She didn't wear makeup or dye her hair and always wore pants and boots. I liked her because she was nice to us kids and smiled all the time. I knew she liked us, but I think she liked Bob more.

Anna May had a son named Tommy who was a teenager and wasn't nice to anyone. He was tall and wore a cowboy hat; everyone in Texas wore cowboy hats, even some of the girls. His hair was always messed up, and he didn't talk much.

Anna May's dairy farm was a few miles down the road from our house. It was big, like the ones we passed on the way to school. She had lots of animals on her farm and made money selling milk from her dairy cows and wool from her sheep. She had more sheep than you could count. She had chickens and cats too. The farm didn't have any dogs; Anna May said it was because dogs chased sheep.

Vance and Valorie found clothes they liked in the church box. Valorie pulled out a pleated skirt. It was dark blue with a broken zipper, but a safety pin would fix it. Safety pins often came in handy. She also found a sweater the color of pea soup. I liked pea soup but not for a sweater. Vance found a pair of long pants in perfect condition, but they were too big around his waist. A safety pin fixed that too. Vance ate a lot, but he was still a beanpole.

Vincent and I ended up wearing stuff we already had because there wasn't anything in the box that fit. I decided to wear my white blouse with anything I had that was clean. Once again, I wished I still had my black patent leather shoes. I felt dressed up when I wore those special shoes.

⁂

By the time we got to Anna May's house, we were starving. She had a big two-story house and only two people lived in it. Tommy was lucky that he and his mom could afford such a nice house. Bob walked up to the porch then knocked on the door, holding a bunch of flowers in his arms. We stood quietly behind him.

When Anna May opened the door, she looked prettier than I had ever seen her. A red ribbon was holding her hair back and she had light pink lipstick on. She wore a skirt and blouse with a red belt around her waist, not overalls and boots. She looked beautiful.

Anna May got a big smile on her face when Bob handed her the flowers. I remembered when Bob handed Mom flowers at the coffee shop. That was the last time I'd seen my mother. I hoped the flowers didn't mean we'd be leaving Texas soon.

The table was set with matching plates and glasses. The silverware was shiny and lying on cloth napkins with lace around the edges. I would make sure not to get my napkin dirty. Licking my lips would work just as well.

I heard music, and it wasn't coming from a radio. Anna May had a real record player and was playing Frank Sinatra. I loved Elvis Presley and wondered if she had his records too.

The living room had beautiful furniture made of leather and a television a lot bigger than the sisters' TV. There were thick rugs on the floor and fancy pillows on the couch. Everything was neat and clean.

The whole house was filled with the smell of delicious food. There was cornbread with melted butter and steaks that looked so juicy my mouth watered. The last time I'd felt this excited about eating dinner was at Grandma Phyllis's house. She'd cooked for us all the time.

The big fire in the fireplace made Anna May's house cozy and warm. She had two bathrooms inside the house, one upstairs and one downstairs. She told us to make ourselves comfortable, so we sat on the couch quietly; we were on our best behavior. I wished I lived there.

Anna May put Bob's flowers in a beautiful vase and then placed them on the dinner table. Now everything was perfect. This was my dream house.

She called us to the table and showed us where to sit. The table was filled with more food than we could possibly eat. I hoped she'd let us take some home. Not only was there steak and cornbread but she'd also made black-eyed peas, mashed potatoes, fresh string beans, and salad. She said the salad and string beans came from her garden.

The best would come last. She had a big bowl of giant red strawberries that were also from her garden, which she was going to serve with real whipped cream made from her cows' milk. I thought whipped cream only came in a can.

She told me she had so many strawberries she had to can them. I wasn't sure why it was called "canning," since the fruit was in glass jars.

"I can teach you how to do it if you like," Anna May said.

I nodded eagerly. "Will you teach me how to make whipped cream too?" I asked. I wanted to learn to cook everything. I wanted to be a good cook like my sister.

When we were in our assigned seats, I whispered to Vincent to remember not to put elbows on the table, and to chew with his mouth closed. My mother said it wasn't polite to eat with your mouth open or talk when it was full. I taught this to Vincent. I taught him everything Mom taught me, and he always listened and did what I said.

Bob sat at one end of the dinner table, and Tommy sat at

the other. Anna May sat next to Bob and I sat next to Anna May. Every now and then, she would reach over and hold my hand under the table. Her hands were rough like a man's hands. She did everything around the farm. She planted vegetables, picked fruit, milked cows, cut the wool off the sheep, and chopped wood for the fireplace. I was sure that was the reason her hands felt like they did. I didn't care, because I liked it when she held my hand. Valorie and Vance sat across from Anna May, and Vincent was squeezed in between Tommy and me.

Bob told everyone to hold hands and bow their heads. Tommy didn't want to hold hands or bow his head.

For the first time ever, Bob said grace. I didn't even know he knew the words to "Bless Us, O Lord." I thanked God for all the food and for Anna May. The second we said, "Amen," the food was passed around.

Anna May and Bob were whispering and laughing about something, but the four of us were too busy eating to care what they were talking about. The food was so yummy, and we were all having such a good time—well, everyone except Tommy. He wasn't talking or smiling at anyone, and he didn't have good manners, either. He ate with his mouth open, and his elbows were on the table. His hair was messed up and his clothes were dusty.

After dinner, while we were having our strawberries with whipped cream, Bob said he had an announcement: he and Anna May were getting married. We kids started clapping and jumping up and down in our seats, but not Tommy. He stood up, didn't say a word, grabbed his cowboy hat, and left the house, slamming the door behind him. I heard his truck taking off out of the driveway, wheels spinning as he pulled out. I knew that sound. We'd gotten stuck in the mud with our truck once, and it had made that same spinning noise.

After Tommy left, Anna May asked us if we'd like to live there. We all said, "Yes!" We couldn't wait to live in this perfect house that had animals, lots of food, and inside bathrooms. *I guess the flowers don't mean we're leaving*, I thought.

Vance asked Anna May if we could bring our dog Fleas.

"Only if he doesn't chase sheep," she said. "Dogs that chase sheep are put down."

"Down where?" I asked.

"That means they have to be shot," she said.

My eyes got big and my mouth fell open.

Vance's eyes filled with tears. "No!" he screamed.

I promised Anna May Fleas wouldn't chase her sheep. We told her Fleas didn't chase anything except bad people. He was the best watchdog in the world, and he was part of our family. I told her not to worry, we'd keep him tied up if she wanted us too.

She smiled and said, "Okay."

I was happy Bob and Anna May were getting married. I liked feeling like a real family, and I was especially happy we got to keep Fleas.

*Thank you, God*, I thought.

## Chapter 21:

# YOU DON'T CHASE SHEEP

We left our small, broken-down farmhouse and moved in with Anna May. I could not have been happier. We had our own beds with thick, fluffy quilts and delicious food cooked for us every day. I didn't think there was anything Anna May couldn't do, just like my mother. I got to help her cook dinner, and she taught me the right places to put knives and forks when setting the table. We always had fresh strawberries or leftovers to snack on whenever we got hungry, and fresh milk and eggs all the time.

Vincent was in charge of collecting the eggs every day. I had to help him, of course. I was no longer worried about going hungry and even made my lunch with bread that was better than Barbara Ann's—it was homemade. We helped Anna May milk the cows, pick vegetables, and clean the house. All our chores were more fun than work, not like at St. Clara's.

I loved getting up early to help Anna May load the delivery truck with cases of bottled milk. We were ready to leave every morning before the sun came up. I used a flashlight when we delivered the milk to every house in town. Anna May slowed the truck down, and I jumped out and put milk on people's porches. She told me how many bottles to leave at each house. Some houses got eggs too. I always knew who had children, because they got the most bottles of milk. It was like they were getting a surprise every morning when they opened their doors.

Anna May told me she loved having a daughter. I told her I loved her too, but I had a mother and she would come to get us one day. Anna May smiled. I thought they'd like each other.

---

It was a long winter, and a few of the sheep had their babies early. Anna May said those babies would die because spring was late, and it was too cold. We went out one morning to try to save a few of the lambs and took Fleas with us. He helped us find the babies left by their mothers. We picked up one of the babies that was still alive and wrapped it in a blanket. When we got into the truck, Fleas lay close to the lamb like he was trying to keep it warm. Anna May said Fleas was a good dog.

As soon as we got home, we put the lamb next to the furnace in the kitchen. I got to feed it with a special baby bottle, and we saved it. Fleas watched the baby lamb all day and all night, protecting it on the back porch. When spring finally came, the lamb was able to join the rest of the sheep, but Fleas continued to watch after it anyway.

One day, I went to Bob because Tommy was being really mean to Vincent and Vance. The day before, Tommy had made Vance stand on a stool with his pants pulled up as high as they would go. Vance had cried and asked if he could get down. I'd kicked Tommy in the leg, and he'd pushed me. I'd fallen over a chair, landed on an electric heater, and burned my stomach.

I showed Bob the burn. It looked like a tick-toe right above my belly button.

"Just ignore Tommy," Bob said. "We need to stay with Anna May a little longer."

I didn't understand what he meant. I thought we were going to live there, and they were going to get married. I was confused again. Why had Bob said that? I hadn't told Anna May about Tommy pushing me, because I didn't want her to get mad and not marry Bob.

I heard Bob talking to Anna May about borrowing money from the bank. He told her they needed to start a new business because he didn't want his wife working so hard anymore, and Anna May agreed. I think she would have agreed with anything Bob said. She told me how much she loved us and our father, and that until she met Bob, she'd never loved anyone except her husband who'd died—then she'd hugged me. She was happy, and I was happy too.

---

We went to church every Sunday. Every Saturday night, Anna May curled my hair with little pieces of rags. The first time she did this, Vance and Vincent laughed at me. I had little knots all over my head. Anna May said, "Just wait until you see what it looks like in the morning." When Anna May took the rags out on Sunday morning, my hair looked beautiful, with curls like Shirley Temple. I loved Shirley Temple. Valorie's and my dresses were already washed and ironed by the time we got up Sunday mornings, and we never even had to ask. Tommy never came with us to church.

One Sunday, Anna May had curled her hair too and had on a new dress. She hardly ever wore dresses because she was always working on the farm. This dress was pretty, with little blue flowers all over it and lace around the bottom, like her slip was showing. She had on lipstick and wore black patent leather shoes. I wanted to ask her where she got those shoes. *I'll do that when Bob isn't around*, I thought.

Bob and Anna May held hands and kissed a lot. When they did, we sang, "Anna May and Daddy, sitting in a tree, k-i-s-s-i-n-g, first comes love, then comes marriage, then comes a baby in a baby carriage!" We laughed so much, and Bob didn't even get mad.

Bob said we were having a breakfast celebration at Cathy's Corner Café because Anna May had good news. She was able to get the money from the bank to start their new business, using the dairy farm as collateral. I knew that word; I'd thought it meant something bad, but now I realized it could be good too, because Bob and Anna May were both excited. I was hoping the new business didn't mean we were going to get rid of the sheep, cows, and chickens.

"What kind of business are you getting?" I asked.

"I'm going to open a used car lot," he said.

He'd sold cars in the past, so I figured it was a good idea.

We ate pancakes with lots of butter and syrup at Cathy's Corner Cafe. Anna May's pancakes were much better, but I didn't tell the nice waitress that. Anna May put her homemade butter and jam on our pancakes, and sometimes even her whipped cream. I never thought I'd rather eat at home instead of a restaurant. It was a happy Sunday.

When we got home, Tommy's truck was blocking the

driveway. Anna May yelled for him to move it, but no one answered. We all went into the house to change out of our church clothes.

I heard Vance outside, calling for Fleas. Fleas usually came running to us whenever we drove up. A few minutes later, Vance came in saying he thought Fleas had run away. I told him that was impossible, Fleas would never do that because he loved us too much. I told Vance we would find Fleas, but he needed to change his clothes before he could go out and look. Vance asked me to go with him.

Once we had our play clothes on, we started out the door to look for Fleas. Vincent wanted to come too, so I stopped to help him tie his shoes. Vance had a worried look on his face and kept saying, "Let's go, let's go."

Just as we stepped out on the back porch, we heard a gunshot.

Bob and Anna May came running out of the house.

"What are you kids doing?" Bob asked.

"Nothing," I said, "we're just on our way to find Fleas."

Bob looked at Vance and Vincent. "You two go into the house with Valorie."

Suddenly, we saw Tommy coming from the upper pasture. Anna May ran up to him and said something. I couldn't hear their conversation, but I did hear Tommy say, "He was chasing sheep." Then Anna May slapped Tommy across his face.

Tommy handed her the gun and stomped away. I heard his truck back out of the dirt driveway fast, the way he always did when he was mad. The tires spun, and dust flew everywhere.

Anna May turned slowly toward Bob and me with tears in her eyes. I felt that sick feeling in my stomach as I ran past her and Bob in the direction Tommy had come from. I ran and ran. Then I saw poor Fleas, tied to a tree. He had blood coming out of his mouth. I knelt beside him, but he was dead. I petted Fleas for the last time.

I walked back into the house feeling like I was waking up from a nightmare, except it was real. I told Vance I'd looked everywhere for Fleas and couldn't find him; he must have run away. Vance started crying like he was in pain.

I turned and left the house. I didn't want to live there anymore.

A few days later, when Anna May was in the cow barn, hooking up the milking machines, we packed up everything we owned and left without saying good-bye. I didn't ask Bob why or where we were going, and I didn't care. Vance had stopped eating, and he cried all the time. It wasn't the same without Fleas.

Bob had a lot of money in his pocket. He traded our old truck for a nicer truck with a front and backseat so we didn't have to ride in the bed of the truck anymore, and said we were leaving Texas.

That was fine with me.

## Chapter 22:

# COLORED ONLY

We were on the move again. "It's time for a change of scenery," Bob said as we headed to who knew where; it was the first time I'd agreed with him. Anna May's dairy farm was the farthest thing from my mind, and no one mentioned her name again. Vance just stared out the window with tears running down his cheeks.

It was 1962. I was eleven years old.

Valorie sat up front with Bob so she could read the map we'd picked up from the Flying Red Horse. That was my favorite gas station because it had a Flying Red Horse ride out front that cost a nickel. Vincent loved it even though he was almost six. We hadn't had time to ride it this time, though, because Bob was in a hurry.

He was always in a hurry.

I sat between Vance and Vincent in the backseat, and they took turns lying on my lap. We drove for two days and two nights, stopping only to get gas and go to the bathroom.

Every time we got out to use the restrooms Vance would cry, and I knew it was because he missed Fleas. We ate potato chips, crackers, and candy bars. We drank Yoo-hoo chocolate milk and Coke until our stomachs ached.

It was early in the morning when we finally got to where we were going. The sign said Biloxi. I didn't know how to say the word, so I asked Bob.

"Stop asking questions," he said. "I'm thinking."

His rudeness didn't bother me anymore, but I hoped he was thinking of a good place to eat and sleep.

In every new town, Bob made friends right away; everyone seemed to like him. Our mom had always said our father could sell a dead man life insurance. After almost three years of living on the road, I finally understood what she meant. Dead men don't need life insurance! She meant Bob could convince anybody of anything—even dead people.

After talking with Bob, kind people would give us free food or a free place to live. We even spent the night in a church once because the pastor felt sorry for us. Being kind is one of God's laws: "Do unto others as you would have them do unto you." We met a lot of good people while we traveled all over the county, but our father wasn't one of them. I could name so many of God's commandments Bob broke.

Valorie said we were finally in Mississippi. Mississippi was a long name, but easy to spell because you only had to remember four letters. We turned into the parking lot of a diner called Grandma's Kitchen, our first real stop in over two days. I couldn't wait to get out of the car. We were hungry and were finally going to have hot food! I wished the diner was our American grandmother's kitchen.

There were beautiful trees all around the diner. Mississippi had lots of beautiful trees but there was one kind that was everywhere. Bob said they were called weeping willows because they looked like they were crying. Their leaves and branches hung toward the ground, covering their face like a green veil. I loved those trees. They made me think of my mother; she was beautiful, and probably weeping, too.

We entered the diner, walking close behind Bob. He winked at the waitress and said, "How about a table, beautiful, for me and my brood?"

"What does 'brood' mean?" I asked, but he ignored me. My mother had always answered my questions; she said asking questions was how a person learned. I knew by now that Bob enjoyed hurting my feelings.

We scooted ourselves into a shiny red booth shaped like a horseshoe. A small jukebox sat on the table, and I wanted to ask Bob for a nickel but not before he got his coffee. The instructions said you could pick three songs with your nickel; I planned to pick Elvis Presley three times.

The waitress handed each of us a menu, except Vincent. I already knew what Vincent wanted: pancakes and hot chocolate with lots of whipped cream. I asked Bob if we could order anything we wanted. I always worried Bob didn't have enough money, so I waited to see what he ordered.

Bob ordered steak and eggs with coffee. That meant he had money, so I ordered eggs with bacon, hash browns, and a chocolate milk shake. I looked over at Bob to see if he thought I was ordering too much, but he was busy looking at the map. Valorie and Vance ordered Pigs in a Blanket; that was a funny name. We could hardly wait until our food came. I flipped through the titles on the jukebox, looking for three Elvis Presley songs.

The diner was packed. Bob always said the best places to eat were where you saw lots of trucks, but I didn't think that was true because the truck stops in Texas never had anything good to eat.

When the food came, we all clapped. The waitress looked at us funny and said, "You kids sure must be hungry." Then she looked at Bob, but he ignored her. I bet if she were pretty, he wouldn't have.

Halfway through breakfast, I needed to go to the bathroom. I asked the waitress where it was, and she pointed toward the back. I didn't know why Bob had called her beautiful, because she was old like Grandma Phyllis. Anyway, on my way to the back, I saw two drinking fountains and stopped at the first one for a quick drink. As I was bending my head to drink, someone grabbed my shoulder. I jumped and looked behind me and there was a big man pulling me away with his big hand.

"Can't you read?" He pointed to the sign above the water fountain. It read "Colored Only."

I didn't understand what that meant so I stood there staring at him, not knowing what to say. I wanted to say, "Yes I can read," but no words came out. I forgot about going to the bathroom and walked quickly back to our booth. I wanted to ask Bob what "Colored Only" meant but knew better. I wasn't going to give him a chance to say I was stupid.

I whispered the question into Valorie's ear. She looked at the sign over the water fountain and whispered back that she didn't know either.

Valorie not knowing made me feel better, because she was smart. Once, Valorie read a small dictionary from cover to cover. We drove for days, and every day she read words to us and then told us what they meant. She almost always knew the answers to my questions.

I wanted to know why that big man had stopped me. Who drank from that fountain? What was Colored? While

I was eating my breakfast, I kept my eye on the water fountain. When Bob got up to ask the man at the cash register a question, I snuck a few sips of his coffee while still looking at the fountain. Someone must use it, but no one did. The only fountain being used was the one under the "Whites Only" sign. I drank almost all of Bob's coffee and hoped the waitress would fill the cup before Bob got back. I loved coffee with lots of cream and sugar, and you could drink as much as you wanted, because refills didn't cost extra money.

I really had to go to the bathroom now. I checked to make sure the big man wasn't around and walked as fast as I could to the back of the diner. This time I walked past the water fountains without even glancing at them.

When I got to the restrooms, there was that word again: "Colored." I waited a minute, then took my chances with Whites Only, because I didn't dare try Colored again.

When I pushed through the bathroom door, there was a waitress standing in front of the mirror. She was much prettier than our waitress.

"Is this the right restroom for kids?" I asked.

She looked at me funny, like she didn't understand my question.

"I thought maybe the Colored restroom was for special people," I said.

"Are you a Yankee?" she asked.

Now I was feeling confused. "What's a Yankee?"

I think she saw I really didn't know, because she said, "Darlin', 'Colored' means Negro. You should always use facilities for white people."

"But I'm not white, I'm Filipino," I said.

She looked annoyed; I knew that look only too well. Then she said, "There are two types of people, missy, niggers and white people." She smoothed down her apron, checked her lipstick with her finger, and, without looking at me, walked out of the bathroom.

I thought of Mr. Jackson, the janitor I'd worked for at my school in Florence. He'd told me he was a Negro, but I didn't understand what "Colored" or "niggers" had to do with the bathrooms and water fountains. Why were they separated? Maybe it was because Negros were poor. As I headed back to our table, I was still confused. I decided to ask Valorie if she knew who nigger people were and if they were from Mississippi.

When I got to our booth, Bob was still at the cash register talking to the same man, and his coffee cup was full again. The man was drawing something on a napkin.

Bob looked over at us and said, "Let's go."

*Go where?* I thought. I wanted to play Elvis on the jukebox. I took my napkin and wrapped up all the extra pieces of toast and packs of jelly for later. Then I gulped down Bob's coffee before grabbing Vincent's hand. We were off again, and I hoped it wouldn't be an all-night trip.

---

"Where are we going?" Valorie asked Bob when we got in the truck.

He handed her the napkin the man had drawn on. "Read the directions."

I could read but Valorie was the best reader. Bob never called her stupid.

We were headed to place called Jackson. Jackson, Mississippi.

## Chapter 23:

# ESTHER

In Jackson, Mississippi, we moved into a small trailer in a large trailer park, but not the kind of park you play in. It was a place with broken-down trailers lined up next to each other; they reminded me of the 18-wheelers at the truck stops. Ours had one bedroom where the four of us slept. Since leaving St. Clara's, we'd felt safer sleeping together.

Because our trailer was so small, Bob and his friends would send us outside when they came over. Most of the time we found stuff to do until dark, and then we'd go back to the trailer and straight to bed. The bedroom was our hiding place, our safe place.

The trailer park had a building with showers and laundry, but nothing seemed to work, so we filled a bucket with water and washed up outside, like the maids did in the Philippines. The people at the park were poor like us, and some were even poorer; you could tell by their trailers.

I didn't like living in the trailer park because it had trash and broken-down cars everywhere. The weeping willows surrounding the trailer park were the only pretty things around. I talked to the trees all the time and pretended my mother had sent them to protect us, and I told Vincent they were our friends. Bob promised we'd move as soon as he got a job.

One day, Bob brought a lady named Esther to our trailer. I'd seen her before because she lived in the trailer park too. They stepped up into our trailer holding hands.

Esther was younger than most of the ladies Bob went out with, and really skinny too. Bob opened a beer and shared it with her. They kissed for a while, and then she asked Bob, "Can I buy some sexy clothes?"

I wondered what kind of clothes those were.

"You can buy whatever you want," Bob said. He looked at us. "You kids get ready; we are going shopping!"

We didn't go shopping very often, so we were excited. I thought it was probably because he'd gotten a new job. We were going to Dillard's department store, where Bob said we could buy one thing each.

Dillard's was a huge store with lots of floors. This store had everything, not just clothes. There was stuff for kitchens and bathrooms, toys, books, and furniture. Bob winked at Esther and said, "Get whatever you want, baby," then patted her on her butt. Why was he calling her baby, and why did she get more than one thing?

---

When we got to Dillard's, Bob said he was taking the boys to the men's department. He told Valorie and me to go with Esther so she could help us pick out what we needed.

I didn't need Esther to help me. She wasn't my mother.

Off we went in opposite directions.

Esther looked at Valorie. "It's time you got a bra," she said. "You're twelve now."

Val made an angry face, but together we followed Esther to the women's area, and for the first time Valorie and I saw women's lingerie. This was where you bought underwear, pajamas, and bras too.

There were soft and silky bras and underwear in all colors. I didn't know underwear could be so fancy. *Why?* I wondered. *No one sees it anyway*. I thought I'd get a pair of silky white ones because mine were ripped in the back. Walking around, I saw some pretty pajamas and thought I should get them instead. I picked a soft, warm, blue pair. Esther took Valorie to look at bras. I never wanted to wear a bra.

Esther held up a white one and handed it to Valorie. My sister grabbed it without saying a word. I could tell she didn't like Esther. I didn't either.

Esther walked over to look at nightgowns. They came in lots of colors and sizes. Some were short with lace all over, and others were long, like a fancy dress. With all that material, I couldn't imagine how they would be comfortable to sleep in. Esther chose a nightgown that was light pink and see-through; it was the most beautiful thing I'd ever seen. Esther said it was sexy. She kept saying that word, but I didn't know what it meant.

The nightgown had a matching long-sleeved coat that was see-through too, with fur all along the opening. I didn't think it could keep anyone warm. Valorie didn't like the nightgown and made a face at Esther when she wasn't looking.

"I'm buying it to surprise Bob," Esther said.

"Why?" I asked. "He isn't going to wear it."

She laughed and said I'd understand when I grew up.

Esther pulled a bunch of money from her purse and paid for Valorie's bra, my blue pajamas, and her pink negligée. She said negligée was French for a sexy nightgown.

"Are pajamas sexy?" I asked.

"No," Esther said.

I was glad my pajamas were warm and not sexy.

I thanked Esther for the pajamas, but Valorie didn't thank her for the bra. Esther said, "Don't thank me, it's your father's money." Now that was a shock. She was carrying Bob's money? He must have gotten a really good job. He was always saying he didn't have a dime to his name, but I knew that wasn't true because cigarettes were thirty-five cents and he bought them every day.

When we finished paying, we looked for Bob and the boys. On the way, Esther stopped at the shoe department. My heart started racing; maybe now was my chance to finally get some black patent leather shoes. I followed Esther into Lady's Shoes. Valorie came with us but sat in a chair and read her book. Val always had a book with her and would sometimes read the same book over and over.

While Esther was looking at some high-heeled slippers, I looked for a pair of black patent leather shoes. I asked the sales lady if they had any and she said yes, then showed me some shiny black high heels. I told the lady I wanted children's shoes, so she pointed downstairs and said, "Children's Department."

Esther bought the high-heeled slippers. They had a fuzzy ball on top, the same color as the fur on her sexy negligée. I asked Esther if we could go downstairs to children's wear so I could buy a pair of shoes too. She said there wasn't any money left.

I didn't know why Esther needed slippers with high heels when you couldn't even wear them outside. I wished I hadn't gotten the pajamas. I wanted black patent leather shoes more. I decided to ask Bob if he had any more money.

Esther handed me her bags. "Carry them," she said.

That made me mad; I wasn't her maid. I should have said no but didn't because saying no always got me in trouble with Bob. Soling carried Mom's bags, but they loved each other.

I was also mad that Esther had spent all the money on her stuff. Valorie asked Esther if she could buy a book, and she got the same answer I had. It wasn't fair. Grownups got to do whatever they wanted; no one told them no.

Now that there was no money left, we looked for Bob and the boys again. I spotted Vincent first. He came running toward me yelling, "Look at me, Mommy!" He was wearing the cutest little US Navy outfit with a white hat to match. The shirt and pants were navy blue with white strips and a tie. Vance had on a green US Army outfit like the ones the soldiers at Fort Hood wore. He pointed to the word Army over the pocket and showed me the stripes on his arm that meant he was a sergeant. Vance was especially excited because playing army with his green army men was his favorite thing to do and now he looked just like them. The boys were so proud marching around the store in their uniforms.

"What did you get?" Bob asked.

Valorie didn't want to show Bob her new bra, but I showed him my pajamas. Esther had wanted me to get pink ones like her negligée, but I didn't like pink and I didn't like Esther.

"And what did you get?" Bob asked Esther.

"It's a surprise," she said.

Vance in his favorite Army outfit

Vincent, age 5

Bob and Esther were acting silly around each other. I was jealous of Esther, not because Bob liked her but because he gave her more stuff than he'd ever given us.

Then Bob took us to Shakey's Pizza, and I stopped being mad.

---

When we got back to the trailer, Esther and Bob started smoking cigarettes and drinking beer while she sat on his lap. The more beer they drank, the more they kissed.

Esther asked Bob if he wanted to see his surprise. Bob said, "Yes!"

I didn't know why a nightgown with stupid furry slippers would be a surprise. I was sure Bob was going to be mad at Esther for spending so much money on them.

Because the trailer had only one bedroom, Bob slept in the front of the trailer where the kitchen table folded into a bed. The blanket and pillow were under the seats. It was a good thing he didn't sleep in our room, because he always came in late and there wasn't any room for him anyway.

Vincent was starting to get tired and I was tired of watching Bob kiss Esther, so I told them that Vincent and I were going to bed. Valorie and Vance wanted to stay up to play Go Fish. Bob told us to do whatever we wanted, but he was taking Esther to the bedroom. He told me to fold down the kitchen table and sleep there.

Right then, I hated Esther and wanted her to go home, but I knew she couldn't go home because when we were at Dillard's she told me she'd run away because she hated her mother and stepfather. I'd told Esther she should never hate her mother because they were the people who loved us most. She said she wished her mother was dead, like mine. I told her she was wrong; my mother wasn't dead, and she was coming soon. Esther told me I was naïve. I told her I wasn't, thinking that I'd ask Valorie what naïve meant later.

We never should have gone shopping. I wanted to take back the fancy nightgown and all our presents. I wanted to sleep in our bedroom. I was so mad at Esther! Didn't she know that was where we slept?

Bob and Esther went into our room and pulled the sliding door closed. We slept on the kitchen table.

⬩●⬩

The next morning, Esther and Bob woke up late. We'd already had our breakfast, and I hadn't saved them any. Bob put the coffee on for Esther and told us to make sure to wish Esther a happy birthday when she got up. They were getting ready to go out to do something special to celebrate.

"It's a big birthday for Esther," he said.

What else was he going to give her? He'd already bought her that dumb negligée and slippers. Valorie, Vance, and Vincent wished Esther a happy birthday. I wished she wouldn't come back.

Bob always forgot our birthdays. He mixed them up every year, and I had to remind him whose birthday it was.

After Bob and Esther left, I went into the bedroom and cut pieces of the pink negligée with Bob's razor. I don't know why I did it, except I think I hated Esther, even on her sixteenth birthday.

## Chapter 24:

# NOT A DIME TO YOUR NAME

Tomorrow would be Father's Day and Valorie wanted to do something special for Bob. Vance thought Pabst Blue Ribbon beer would be a good gift, and Vincent wanted to buy Dad a bike because his truck was always out of gas. Valorie called both of them stupid and said we didn't have any money for presents.

I hated it when Valorie called them stupid because Bob called me stupid all the time and it didn't feel good. I made her say sorry, and I told Vincent he was the smartest boy in the world and if we had the money, a bike would be a good idea.

Then I suggested a Father's Day card. Vance and Vincent clapped and shouted, "Yeah!"

I had a dime in my secret box but didn't know if it was enough to buy a card, so I told everyone to hunt through the trailer for loose change.

"Like an Easter egg hunt?" Vincent asked. We'd done that once at a church; most of the kids had thrown the colored hardboiled eggs in the trash and only kept the chocolate eggs, but I'd saved all my hardboiled Easter eggs—they were my favorite.

Vance found three shiny pennies, Vincent found two broken crayons, and I found a piece of red ribbon and an almost dried-out bottle of Elmer's glue. Valorie didn't find any money but in the back of the cabinet she found a box of Betty Crocker Cake mix with a picture of a yellow cake with chocolate frosting on it.

I had a great idea! Valorie could make a cake, and I would make a Father's Day card using some of the stuff we found; that way we wouldn't need money! Bob would be so surprised; plus, we'd all get cake!

Vance and Vincent liked my idea and started clapping and jumping up and down.

Valorie opened the box of cake mix and saw there wasn't any frosting. I didn't understand why the box would show a frosted cake and not have frosting. What were we going to do now? We didn't have the money to buy frosting, and the cake wouldn't look like a cake without it.

"We don't need frosting," Valorie said.

"Yeah we do," Vance said, "all cakes need frosting."

Valorie thought for a minute, then smiled. "We can put small flowers all over the top of the cake! It will be pretty, like the wedding cake with candy flowers that I saw in a magazine."

Our plan was to surprise Bob with a beautiful cake and a card. We worked together to get everything done before he got home. Val got all the stuff out for the cake, and I looked for a pan but couldn't find one and started to worry. Then Valorie pulled out our cast iron frying pan and said, "This will work!"

I wasn't sure how a frying pan was going to make a cake. Frying pans were for making bacon and eggs. But I trusted Valorie, she always made things work.

I took a piece of paper from my school notebook and asked Vincent for the crayons he'd found. He wanted to help so I told him to draw a picture for our dad; it would be a good gift.

Vance's job was to take out the trash, empty the ash-trays, sweep the trailer floor, and be our lookout, in case Bob got home early. Vance liked sneaking around outside looking for Bob. He lay on the ground behind bushes, just like GI Joe.

I was trying to think of something to write on the front of the card. Or maybe I'd draw a picture or write a poem? I couldn't decide. Most Father's Day cards said stuff about how much you loved them or what a great dad they were. Bob was neither.

When Vincent finished with Bob's picture, I gave him another piece of paper to practice writing his name. A few weeks earlier, I'd taught him to write his first and last name. Now he could sign the card himself, like the rest of us. I was also teaching him how to tie his shoes.

I was on my third piece of paper and nothing sounded right. I hated wasting my school paper. Then I had another idea. I went to my secret box and took out the last two nickels I'd been saving for an emergency.

I wrote in big red letters across the front of the card, *Don't Ever Say You Don't Have a Dime to Your Name*; when Bob opened the card, he'd see two nickels glued inside. Under the nickels I wrote, *Happy Father's Day!* I took the red ribbon I'd found and the last of the Elmer's glue and stuck it around the edge of the card. The ribbon matched the red crayon. It was perfect!

I drew stars on the inside and outside of the card, and then I put X's and O's below the two nickels. We all signed our names as neatly as possible.

*Valorie*
*Veronica*
*Vance*
*Vincent*

I felt proud; the card looked better than the ones at the drug store.

"Why did you glue the nickels inside the card?" Vincent asked me.

"Because Dad always says, 'I don't have a dime to my name,' and now he can't say that anymore," I said.

"But they're nickels, not dimes," Vincent said.

I told him that two nickels were the same as one dime, but he still didn't get it.

I'd teach him about money some other time.

The trailer smelled so good, and we were getting more and more excited about our surprise. Valorie let Vance and Vincent lick the bowl and spoon. Vincent kept asking if the cake was done, and Vance asked how we'd know. Valorie stuck a toothpick into the middle of the cake and explained that when the toothpick came out clean, the cake was done. Valorie was right, the frying pan worked.

While the cake was cooling, we went out to look for flowers. There were lots of trees around our trailer, but we couldn't find any flowers, so we decided to walk a couple of blocks away from the trailer park.

Just around the corner, there was a row of nice houses. One of them had roses growing in the yard but some were outside of their white fence. As we stood looking at the flowers, Valorie said, "It's okay to take a few of these roses because they aren't in the yard."

I was worried we were going to get in trouble and wanted to knock on the door to ask if we could have a few, but before I got the courage to go up and knock, Valorie picked three roses.

We all took off fast.

My heart raced as I looked around to see if anyone was coming after us. I knew it was stealing, and stealing was a sin. I'd make sure to go to confession the next time I saw a Catholic Church.

There are two kinds of sins: mortal sins and regular, everyday sins, like talking back to your elders or hitting your brother. I wasn't sure which one stealing flowers was, but I hoped it wasn't a mortal sin. You could go to Hell if you died with a mortal sin on your soul.

When we got back to the trailer, Valorie and I gently pulled the petals off the roses, two pink and one yellow. The cake was cool, so we carefully covered the top with the petals. It was beautiful! Valorie was right; she was smart like Mom.

We put the cake on the fold-down table along with the Father's Day card and Vincent's picture of our dog Fleas. Everything looked perfect.

We waited in our spic-and-span trailer for Bob to come home until it started getting late, then we decided to go to bed. Valorie left the front light on for him so he wouldn't miss seeing his surprise. Sometimes Bob got home late on the weekends. I wished I could keep my eyes open to see Bob's face when he saw our cake and card. I knew he would be surprised. Having cake for Sunday breakfast would make Father's Day special, even better than pancakes.

---

We didn't hear Bob come home that night, and when we got up, he wasn't there. We knew he'd come home, though, because there were cigarette butts in the ashtray next to the cake and two empty cans of Pabst Blue Ribbon beer on the table. I didn't see the card, so he must have taken it with him. He didn't eat any of the cake, and the rose petals were wilted and not pretty anymore. Maybe he was waiting for us to get up before eating his cake. Where could he be?

Then I saw our card and Vincent's picture lying on the floor under the fold-down table. I grabbed Vincent's picture and put it on the table before he saw it. I told Vincent that Bob had probably gone to the store and would be back soon.

When I picked up the Father's Day card, it felt light. I opened it and saw that the two nickels had been torn off, ripping the back of my card. We didn't know what to think, so we just sat in silence.

Valorie picked off all the stolen petals, and we ate Bob's cake for breakfast.

Now *I* didn't have a dime to my name.

## Chapter 25:

# THE FISH CAMP

It was a hot, sweaty afternoon at the fish camp. There was no shade except in the trailer or the bait house and both seemed hotter than outside because you couldn't feel the light breeze. I wished Bob had picked a different job and a better place to live than this fish camp. This was where we'd moved to after the trailer park. We'd picked up and left quickly, just like we always did.

When we left Mississippi, Bob drove all night until we reached Galveston. We stopped for breakfast at a coffee shop, and Bob started talking with two men at the table next to us—telling them we were new in town, and he was looking for a job and a place to live. I was glad to be eating but hated being back in Texas. Bob said Texas was bigger than most countries, so we shouldn't worry about running into Tommy or Anna May. My heart still hurt when I thought about Fleas; I kept him in my prayers every night. I did miss Anna May, her house, and all the good food. It wasn't her fault her son was a murderer. Tommy would go to Hell for what he did, because I knew he wouldn't ask God for forgiveness.

Bob's new friends joined us and told him about a business near the border with enormous potential that was just waiting for the right person to run it. "It will solve both your problems, Bob!" they said. "You can live and work in the same place."

I knew enormous meant big and potential probably had something to do with money; I could tell Bob was interested. While they talked about stuff I didn't understand, we ordered Cokes and sandwiches. My Grandma Phyllis once said, "Your father is a man of all trades and a master of none." That meant he could do lots of different jobs.

When we were done eating, we climbed back into the truck and headed to our new home, a place called Brownsville. Bob was the new owner of a fish camp: Bob's Fish Camp.

The fish camp was a big place, like the farm in Florence, only there weren't any animals or trees. All the fish camp had was lots of dirt, a trailer, and the ocean. Our fish camp was on the Gulf of Mexico. I don't know why it was called Mexico; we were in Texas.

We had no neighbors for miles and didn't go to school. Bob made money by charging people to sit in chairs and fish off the cliff. Besides the trailer we lived in, there was a bait house and a dock with a small motorboat tied to it. Bob taught us to cut bait to sell to the customers. We also sold beer, soda, and bags of Planters peanuts. There weren't many people on weekdays, but on the weekends we were packed. People drove into the camp with their coolers and fishing poles. The real fishermen came early to get the best spots along the edge of the cliff, and some paid extra for a chair down on the dock.

Vincent was never allowed to go down on the dock because he disappeared once, and we thought he fell off and drowned. It was just before dinner, and I went outside to call everyone to the trailer. Vance and Valorie came racing out of the bait house. Bob was inside the trailer making fishing lures he'd sell to the customers to help them catch bigger fish. The lures were beautiful and came in all colors; they reminded me of the dragonflies in Florence. I missed that stream, especially because when we'd played in the clean, cold water we hadn't needed to take a bath when we got home.

It was my night to make dinner. I'd made my usual grilled cheese sandwiches and canned corn. Vincent didn't come in with Valorie and Vance, so I asked where he was. "Don't know," they both said, and they grabbed their seats at the table.

I stuck my head out the trailer door and yelled Vincent's name over and over. I waited a minute, then yelled again. I started to get that sick feeling in my stomach. "You guys were in charge of watching him!" I told Valorie and Vance.

"He didn't want to play, he wanted to be with you in the trailer," they said.

Vincent was almost six now, but I still felt he needed looking after. I'd promised Mom I would keep him safe.

Bob got up from the table and went outside. I heard him yelling for Vincent in his angry voice.

"I wouldn't want to be Vincent when Dad finds him," Vance said.

After a few minutes, I went out to help Bob look. When I got to the bait house, he looked worried and told me to get Vance and Valorie. He ordered us to spread out and cover every inch of the camp, including looking over the edge of the cliff.

The fish camp was big, but it was easy to see from one end to the other because it was flat, except for the small hill where our trailer sat. Vincent was nowhere to be seen. I started crying and yelling Vincent's name as I walked along the cliff. I looked over the edge, being careful not to get too close.

It was getting dark, so Bob put on the lights we used for night fishing. They helped a little but mostly shined off the water.

"I'm going to search the shoreline in the boat," Bob said. "Don't stop looking." He headed down to the dock.

Valorie, Vance, and I stood at the top of the dock with our fingers crossed. I had never been more scared in my life. I took my rosary from around my neck and held it over my heart. I could barely breathe. I closed my eyes and said, "Please God, don't let Vincent be dead."

Bob had just started the motor when I heard him say, "What the hell are you doing in there?" Our prayers were answered. Bob had found Vincent. *God heard me!*

Vincent was in the front of a boat, buried under the life jackets. He said he never got to go anywhere and wanted to ride in the boat. Boy, did Bob get mad! He spanked Vincent hard and dragged him by his arm up the dock. Vincent cried the whole way.

I didn't want to spank Vincent; I just wanted to hug and kiss him. He was my responsibility until Mom found us.

Once we got back to our trailer, I made him promise to never do that again. I told him to promise, in the name of God, to never go near the dock or the bait house without me. He kept sobbing and saying, "I'm sorry! I promise in the name of God!"

I hugged him until he stopped crying.

The bait house was at the top of the dock; that's where we cleaned fish and cut bait. It wasn't really a house; it was more like a small shed. It had a door and two little windows. Inside was a big refrigerator with a giant freezer on top, a tank for live fish, a wooden table and chair where we cut up bait, and a bucket for the fish guts; nothing else fit in the bait house.

We did our chores on weekdays, so we'd be ready for the busy weekends. The chores at the fish camp were not fun. Taking care of customers was hard work, but that I didn't mind because most people were nice. Our main chores—cutting up bait and making sure the bait house was clean—were much worse. Fish guts and scales stuck to the wooden floor, and it took a lot of scrubbing to get them off.

My job was gutting the fish with a sharp knife from its belly to its head. Then Valorie and Vance would cut the fish into small pieces—not too big and not too small. Vincent was too young to use a knife, so his job was putting the bait into small bags. We cut up squid, catfish, mullet, and any other fish the customers didn't want or left behind. The unwanted fish made the best bait for catching bigger fish. We'd sell the customers their own fish for fifty cents a bag! The left-over bags of bait got stuffed into the giant freezer for the next day.

The bottom part of the refrigerator was packed with beer and soda. We weren't allowed to drink even one bottle of Orange Crush or Pepsi, but Bob got to drink all the beer he wanted. I didn't think that was fair.

Bob told us we could make good money from tips if we stayed on our toes. That didn't make any sense to me. Who runs around on their toes?

The best tips came from the people on the dock. Some weekends I would make five dollars in nickels, dimes, and even quarters. We always gave our money to Bob because he needed it to take care of us. Sometimes people would leave tasty fish if they couldn't fit it into their coolers. Valorie was good at cooking fish and we loved it; snapper and flounder were my favorite.

I wished we could go to school but Bob said it was too far away, so we had to be "home schooled," which meant we had to read and practice our handwriting ourselves. There wasn't anything good to read or even paper and pencils to write on, I thought, so how were we going to learn anything?

Valorie taught us words from her pocket dictionary. She made Vance and me memorize three hard words a day. I taught Vincent arithmetic with coins and how to read from magazines.

From Bob's Fish Camp you could see the United States Coast Guard boats. Sometimes they would come to visit us in their speedboats, which went a lot faster than our boat. We loved the Coast Guard guys. They brought us Wrigley's gum and magazines they were finished with. Once, when they were at our fish camp, they taught Vance how to use flags to signal SOS. That meant Save Our Ship. They said we could use the flags to send a signal if we ever needed them.

We didn't have a phone, so that might come in handy.

I liked it when the Coast Guard came to the fish camp. They said we were smart kids and should be in school. I told them we were home schooled. We would let them fish for free, but they only came to talk with Bob. I think they were trying to convince him to take us to the school in town. I heard one of them say, "Home schooling four children is too much for you."

Fish camp, Brownsville, Texas

Bob taught us how to bait a hook, string a fishing pole, reel in a fish, and use a sharp knife, but he didn't teach us anything about reading, writing, or arithmetic.

Once a week, Bob drove our pick-up truck into town. He'd put a large metal container on the back of the truck and fill it with clean drinking water. Today was that day.

We watched the truck coming up the road, kicking clouds of dust behind it, and shouted, "The water is coming! The water is coming!" We started jumping and clapping with joy. Today was bath day. We always looked forward to bath day. Vincent was especially excited because he could play with his plastic PT-109 boat.

When Bob drove into the fish camp, we rushed out with empty bottles in both hands. We filled all the water bottles first; whatever was left in the tank after that was ours to play in. As soon as we finished our chores, we were allowed to get into the tank and bathe. There was running water in the bait house, but it wasn't for drinking, it was for washing our hands or cleaning out the smelly bait house.

The metal container was big enough for the four of us to sit in. We took off our clothes, except our underwear, and played till it was almost dark; then we used soap on our bodies and hair. The clean water felt good.

I washed Vincent's hair last, just before it was time to get out. His hair was long because Bob hadn't cut his hair in a while. Vincent loved his long hair and hid whenever it was time for haircuts. I was glad Bob wanted my hair long.

When we finally climbed out of the tank, our fingers were wrinkled and we were squeaky clean. The water was cold, and we were shivering, but we didn't care. It was fun.

I especially liked smelling clean when it was time for bed. Even my hands smelled good and not like fish guts anymore.

As much as I loved bath day, I hated everything else about Bob's Fish Camp.

## Chapter 26:

# HI HO INN

We were sitting in a restaurant that was so dark you could hardly make out people's faces. The tables didn't have tablecloths, menus, or even silverware, and customers were allowed to move the tables and chairs wherever they wanted.

Bob told us to *stay put* at our table while he bought adult drinks at the bar. The bar was a long table where he made friends and drank beer. I hoped he didn't forget we were there and leave us behind again like he had once when we lived in Florence. That night, one of his friends from Fort Hood finally took us home. This restaurant was so dark, Bob might not see us.

Right next to our small table was a large one that wasn't for eating. It was for playing a game called pool. The table had lots of colorful balls, and two men with long sticks tried to make the balls disappear into holes on the side of the table.

It looked like fun. We wanted to play but it was for adults only, like the long counter where Bob stood.

The music, coming from large boxes on the wall, was so loud we couldn't hear each other talk. I wished they would turn up the lights and turn down the radio.

The men with the long sticks weren't speaking English. It sounded a little like Filipino, but I didn't understand any of the words. A waitress came over and asked us what we were doing there. I proudly told her we were the Slaughter children and were with our father, then pointed to the long counter where Bob was standing. The waitress asked if we wanted something to eat or drink, and we said, "Yes, please."

I asked the waitress why no one was speaking English, and she said because we were south of the border. What did that mean? She walked away before I could ask. She went over to Bob, who was talking to a lady wearing lots of makeup. The waitress said something to him as she pointed toward our table. Bob nodded up and down, then went back to talking to the lady with lots of makeup.

People seemed to be drinking more than eating at this restaurant, and we were the only kids there. Finally, the man from behind the counter came over with four Cokes, which was just what we needed. It was hot and stuffy in the restaurant because everyone was smoking and there were no fans or windows. The man who brought our Cokes had a cigarette in his mouth that flipped up and down as he talked. We didn't understand what he was saying, so we just said, "Thank you."

When we finished our Cokes, Vincent told me he was hungry, so I went to find Bob. I couldn't see him at the counter anymore because the restaurant had gotten really crowded. I pushed through the crowd, excusing myself, as Vincent hung on to the pocket of my pants.

I finally found Bob at the other side of the bar, still talking to the lady with lots of makeup. I had to tap his arm two times before he looked down at me. He had a beer in one hand and his other hand was on the lady's waist. I told him we were hungry and tired and wanted to know when we were going home. He just ignored me and kept drinking his beer.

The lady with lots of makeup bent down to talk to Vincent. She smiled and said, "*Ven, mi corazón*, I'll get you something good to eat." I followed her because she took Vincent's hand. Vincent kept turning around to make sure I was still there.

The woman was speaking English, but it didn't sound like the way we talked. She said, "*Mi nombre es Rosalina*, what is your name?"

I told her our names but wished she would let go of Vincent's hand. Rosalina had a puffy white lace blouse on that looked too small because it was tight and showed her breasts, especially when she bent down to talk to Vincent.

Rosalina, still holding Vincent's hand, walked to the kitchen and yelled something I couldn't understand. After a few minutes, a man came out with a plate full of sandwiches. I was happy we finally had something to eat.

"Can we please have more Cokes?" I asked.

"*Sí*," she said. "I'll send them to your table."

I thanked Rosalina, and then she bent down and gave Vincent a kiss on his cheek. I quickly pulled Vincent's hand from hers and walked back to our table.

I was keeping my eye on Bob to make sure he didn't leave without us. I figured as soon as were done with our sandwiches, I'd go back and remind him that it was time to go home. He still had his arm around Rosalinda's waist, and was sometimes putting his hand on her bottom. He was kissing her and talking in her ear like he had with Esther in Mississippi.

After forever, Bob came over. “Stay where you are,” he said. “I’ll be back shortly, and then we’ll go home.”

I’d heard those words before. “Can we go with you?”

He shook his head. “Stay put!”

I started to get that sick feeling in my stomach.

I watched Bob and Rosalina walk toward the door of the dark restaurant. When Bob opened the door, sunshine came pouring in; then the door closed, and it was dark again.

I didn’t like this restaurant. They only served beer, Coca Cola, and little sandwiches that were just cheese between two slices of bread. I looked around and noticed most of the people were men, and they were staring at us like we didn’t belong there. I wanted to go home; I felt worried and scared that Bob was going to leave us there. I prayed he would come back right away.

The man from behind the bar came to our table and handed us a deck of cards. He still wasn’t speaking English, so we just thanked him again and started playing Go Fish.

---

It was late now. I didn’t know what time it was, but we had been waiting for Bob a long time. Vance was fast asleep, his head on the table. There were two men showing Valorie how to put the colored balls into a triangle on the big green table. The man would bend down and pat Val’s bottom every time she finished. I was glad she was having fun.

Vincent was tired and getting hungry again, so I walked up to the long counter and asked if we could have more sandwiches. The bartender looked at me and shook his head no, then handed me a small bowl of peanuts. I asked him if he knew when our father was coming back. He shook his head again. I knew when Bob said "shortly," it didn't mean anything. He'd probably forgotten us again, and now who was going to take us back to the fish camp?

Finally, Bob came through the door. I could tell it was him by the way he walked, even though you couldn't see his face. It was pitch black outside. Rosalina wasn't with him and the restaurant was almost empty. I ran and hugged him tight, not because I loved him but because I thought he had left us behind.

Vance and Vincent were sleeping with their heads down on the small metal table. I had to shake them hard to get them to wake up. Vincent wanted me to carry him, but he was too heavy, so I asked Bob if he would. Valorie was still at the big table with all the different-colored balls and the two men. Bob picked up Vincent, and I ran over to get her. Valorie showed me a handful of money the men had given her for helping them. It didn't look like real money, but she put it in her pocket anyway.

We all stumbled, half asleep, out to the truck. Vincent's eyes never really opened; it was like he was sleepwalking after Bob put him down, I had to guide him into the backseat.

I was glad to be driving away. As we pulled out of the dirt parking lot, I turned and looked back. All I could see was a sign against the black sky flashing, *Hi Ho Inn . . . Hi Ho Inn . . . Hi Ho Inn.*

Valorie, Vance, and Vincent were asleep before we got to the highway.

I stayed awake, watching the blackness go by. I was thinking of my mother. What was she doing right now? Where could she possibly be?

My eyes were getting heavy and I was about to fall asleep when I saw a bright light ahead. It was a big billboard with lights shining down on it. As we got closer, I realized it was in another language. When we reached the sign, I saw that part of it was in English. It read: YOU ARE NOW LEAVING MEXICO. WELCOME TO TEXAS.

## Chapter 27:

# SOS

It was another hot, boring, Wednesday afternoon at the fish camp. Every day was hot in the summer and the only thing that made it comfortable was a breeze, but today there wasn't even a tiny one. We didn't have one customer, either, which made it twice as boring.

Bob left early and said he was going to visit a friend. We didn't have friends besides the Coast Guard, so I wondered who he was talking about but didn't ask because I already knew the answer—"Mind your own business, Veronica" or "Stop asking so many questions, Veronica." I hoped he would come back with groceries.

The heat made us lazy and tired. None of us wanted to do our chores. We ate cinnamon rolls for lunch because that was all we had left. After we ate, Vance and Vincent chased each other around the camp, playing tag, while Valorie and I sat in the trailer with wet rags around our necks, playing cards. We were supposed to be cutting bait for the weekend, but no one felt like it. I knew Bob would be furious if we didn't cut bait, so we all agreed to play a few more hours, until the sun went down, and then we'd cut bait. We knew Bob always got home late on Wednesdays. Whoever he visited on Wednesdays must not have liked kids, because he never brought them to the fish camp.

Vance and I decided to go down to the dock and play in the boat. Bob called it a dingy. I didn't like that name because it made the boat sound dumb. Since Bob wasn't home, I let Vincent walk down to the dock with me after making him promise to stick to me like glue.

Vance brought fishing lines so we could fish off the boat. We never fished much because we were always too busy cutting bait or making sure the customers had what they needed. Fishing off the boat was going to be fun. When the three of us were seated in the boat, Vance realized he'd forgotten the bait, so I called up to Valorie to bring some from the big freezer. She yelled back, "Okay!"

The bait house was especially stinky and slimy that day because it was hot, and I hadn't cleaned the fish guts off the table and chair. That would be the first chore I'd do when we were done fishing. The freezer was high, so to reach the bait behind the frozen fish you had to stand on the chair.

Our fishing poles were almost ready when Valorie screamed, "HELP ME! HELP ME!"

Her scream sounded like a scary movie when someone was about to be killed. I grabbed Vincent's hand and hauled him out of our boat, and we ran as fast as we could toward the bait house.

When we opened the door Valorie was still screaming and there was blood everywhere. I couldn't see her foot because of all the blood. I didn't know what to do and Bob wasn't home, so I started to pray.

A frozen catfish fin was stuck into the top of Valorie's foot. She hadn't wanted to stand on the chair because she was barefoot and the chair was slippery and covered with fish guts. When she reached up to pull bait out of the freezer, a frozen fish had slipped out of her hand and landed on top of her foot, and the fin had gone through her foot like a nail. I pictured Jesus on the cross, bleeding where the soldiers hammered a nail through his foot. Jesus died. I didn't want my sister to die.

I told Vincent to stay with Valorie while Vance and I ran out of the bait house and back down to the dock. I wished we had a telephone because this was an emergency. Vance and I started jumping up and down, yelling to the Coast Guard across the gulf. We yelled until our throats hurt and waved our arms until we thought they were going to fall off, but the Coast Guard couldn't hear us. We saw them, but they weren't looking in our direction. We had to get their attention before Valorie died! Then Vance remembered that one of the Coast Guard men had taught him how to signal SOS with flags. SOS—Save Our Sister!

Vance grabbed rags out of the dingy and started moving his arms in different directions.

"What are you doing?" I asked.

"Signaling, the way the Coast Guard taught me!" he said.

"They're never going to come," I said. "You're not even using real flags, and you're not doing it right."

Vance ignored me and kept waving the rags.

It was a miracle! The rags worked! Suddenly there were three men in a speedboat heading for our dock. Vance was right! The Coast Guard was coming to help!

We'd left Valorie in the bait house with the fish still in her foot, so when the Coast Guard men got out of their boat, we started yelling, "Please hurry! Our sister is dying!" Then we ran in front of them, calling, "Come quick!"

Vance pushed open the bait house door and the men rushed in behind him, carrying a bag with a big red cross on it. Vincent was sitting next to Valorie, being brave by not crying. One of the Coast Guard men squatted down next to Valorie. It was hot and stinky in the bait house, and I wished I had cleaned it before playing. If I had, Valorie would have stood on the chair instead of trying to reach up high into the freezer. It was my fault Valorie's foot was nailed to the floor. I whispered, "Please, St. Jude, don't let Valorie die."

The Coast Guard man said, "Everything is going to be all right, young lady. We're going to take good care of you." Those were the best words ever, and we all calmed down.

The man had to pull on the frozen fish two times before he was able to unstick Valorie's foot from the wooden floor; then he cut the fish off her foot, leaving the fin in it. Valorie was still crying, but not as loud as before.

"We have to get your sister to sick bay right away," he said.

This was fine with me, as long as it helped Valorie. Bad things kept happening at the fish camp. I was going to tell Bob we should move, even if he got mad.

One of the Coast Guard men asked me where our father was.

I gave my standard answer: "He'll be home soon."

He picked Valorie up and held her like a baby. Her foot was wrapped in bandages, but I could see it was still bleeding. Vance, Vincent, and I followed them back to their boat, which we barely all fit into. It was so exciting, I almost forgot Valorie was hurt.

Once we were in the boat, they asked us lots of questions about Bob. Why we weren't in school? Where did our father work? What time did he leave, and what time did he usually get home?

I was worried I'd say the wrong thing because Bob told us if he got in trouble, the four of us would be separated. We never wanted to be separated, so I told the Coast Guard men Bob had gone shopping for food. It didn't look like they believed me. One of them raised his eyebrow the way Mom used to do when she thought I wasn't telling the whole truth.

In a few minutes, we were at the Coast Guard dock. Once we got out of the speedboat, we got onto the bigger Coast Guard boat. Valorie was still being carried and was taken straight to sick bay. They told us that's where you saw the doctor and got fixed up. Another nice Coast Guard man took Vance, Vincent, and me to the mess hall for something to eat. I didn't know why they called it a mess hall; it looked spic and span to me.

We ate like the three little pigs. We had only eaten cinnamon rolls that day and the Coast Guards' food was really good. They even gave us root beer floats!

When we were done eating everything in sight, a Coast Guard man showed us around the ship. He took us to where the captain lived, where they slept, and where the engine was. This was more fun than going to Disneyland! We weren't bored anymore.

Valorie got stitches in her foot, and two shots. Her foot looked gigantic with all the bandages. I was worried we were going to get in trouble because we didn't do our chores, but instead everyone was nice and said we were brave. One Coast

Guard man told Vance, "Good job, young man, you deserve a medal for saving your sister!" Vance sat up tall and smiled.

The four of us sat on one side of a long table with three Coast Guard guys across from us. They taught us a new card game called War. It was so easy, even Vincent won sometimes.

⸻

It was getting late.

"When will you take us home?" I asked. "I'm sure our dad is back, and he'll be worried."

A man with lots of colorful bars on his jacket came into the mess hall and said, "We can't let you go home until we reach your father."

I was afraid to tell them that on Wednesdays Bob got home late. I also secretly wished Bob wouldn't come so we could stay on the ship a little longer. We had everything we wanted on this ship. We were treated special, and everyone liked us.

I don't know exactly how much later, but finally, two ladies in high heels and a man dressed in a suit came onto the boat. They said we had to go with them. I knew this wasn't good. I prayed Bob would hurry up and get there. I usually prayed that he wouldn't come home unless we needed food or something.

The three strangers asked us lots of questions, just like the Coast Guard had. We told them our father was home every day except today, and that our truck broke down a lot and that was probably why he was late.

Just then, Bob walked in with one of the Coast Guard guys. He grabbed us, and we all hugged him. He looked like he was going to cry when he went over to Valorie and said, "How is my baby girl?"

That was the first time I'd ever heard Bob call any of us baby. I didn't know why he'd said it, but I did know I was happy he was there. I was sure the strangers who'd come to talk to us were the people who would separate us.

One of the ladies stayed with the four of us in the mess hall while the other man and lady stepped out with Bob to talk. We waited in the mess hall a long time. Vincent fell asleep on my lap as I prayed quietly, Valorie complained about the pain in her foot, and Vance had another root beer float.

Finally, Bob came in and said, "We are going home."

Whatever he'd told the lady in high heels and the man in the suit had worked.

Mom was right: Bob could sell a dead man life insurance.

## Chapter 28:

# THE WISHING WELL

It was gone! The Spartan trailer Bob had bought after we left Brownsville was gone!

That beautiful, shiny trailer was the best place we had lived in so far. It was much nicer and bigger than the ones in Jackson, Mississippi, or the fish camp. There was a bedroom in the front of the trailer and one in back. We had a big table for eating and playing cards, and when we were done it folded into a third, bigger bed. The bathroom also had a shower, which was my favorite thing of all.

Bob had traded in our old truck, with the water tank on the back, for the Spartan trailer and a new truck when we arrived in Corpus Christi. In the Philippines, priests always said the words "*corpus Christi*," which mean "body of Christ," before you opened your mouth for communion. You weren't supposed to chew the host because it was God's body, so I always let it melt in my mouth.

Bob sold the fish camp to a man who gave him lots of money the day we left. I was happy to leave but would miss the Coast Guard guys. We weren't able to say good-bye to them. We almost never got to say good-bye when we left a place. Still, the shiny trailer was the answer to one of my prayers. We could move anywhere we wanted and didn't have to pack and unpack anymore or leave things behind.

When we got home from school, however, Bob was packing the truck and the trailer wasn't hooked to the back. What happened to our beautiful trailer? My rosary! My secret box! Bob started shouting, "Hurry up and get the rest of this stuff into the truck." All our belongings were in brown paper bags on the ground. I was in shock! We had just started our new school here in Alabama, and I had a new best friend.

"Where's my rosary?" I asked Bob, but he didn't answer.

Why were we moving again? Where was my secret box? I wanted to cry.

"No more trailers for us!" Bob said. "We're headed to our new house."

What new house? Where was this house? He said we had to leave right away and promised we wouldn't have to move from place to place ever again.

I didn't know whether to believe him or not. But you couldn't question Bob when he was thinking, drinking, angry, or packing. Actually, you could never question him.

I took Vincent's hand and told him to help me put the paper bags in the truck. When I picked up the old army blanket, there was my secret box. *Oh, thank you, St. Jude!* I opened the box and my rosary was safe. I would die if I lost my rosary. I prayed every night that my mother would come get us. I needed my rosary more than anything else.

Bob wasn't lying! After driving all night, we arrived at a small house early in the morning. I couldn't believe it; this was an actual house. How did he know it was here? We got out of the car and went in. It was completely empty but very clean and had a stove and a white refrigerator—tall, but not as big as the one at the fish camp. There were two bedrooms, one for Bob and one for us. The bathroom had a shower and a bathtub, which meant that Vincent could play with his PT-109 boat.

I'd bought that boat for him with my savings from babysitting—a whole dollar. Vincent didn't have any toys, so I went to the 88 Cent Store and saw a big red boat that had PT-109 written on the side. I didn't know what that meant, but it didn't matter because Vincent loved his boat. I even got change from my dollar.

Once we got our belongings out of the truck and into our new house, Bob called us into the empty living room and told us to sit down on the floor. He stared out the window for a long time, then whispered, "Listen carefully."

I didn't know why he was whispering; no one was around.

He told us that if we didn't do exactly what he said, the police would take us away and we wouldn't have this nice house. We would be separated into different families. Bob always said that when he was about to ask us to do something hard or wrong. I thought I wouldn't mind being taken away as long as we were kept together, but that wasn't how it worked. No one wanted four children. Most people only wanted one or maybe two, but never four.

I knew better than to ask why he was telling us this, but I had a feeling it had something to do with the shiny Spartan trailer. We'd left so quickly it had felt like we were running away from somebody—probably someone he owed money to.

"Your last name is Bromley now," Bob said. He made us say our new last name over and over. It wasn't hard to remember because my Grandma Phyllis, in Colorado, had said our step-grandfather's name was Earl Bromley. I'd seen Bromley on my grandfather's tombstone, just below the picture of Golden Boy.

"My name is Veronica Bromley, and I'm adopted." I had to say it after him. Then he made Valorie and Vance repeat after him as well.

The only word I hated more than *poor* was the word *adopted*. I'd spent my time at St. Clara's trying to convince everyone I wasn't adopted. I hated having to pretend I was adopted again.

We all said our names then said we were adopted.

Bob smiled. "No mistakes," he ordered. "It's a matter of life or death."

*What did he mean by that?*

He told us people from the Baptist church were coming to bring us clothes, blankets, dishes, and other donations, and not to speak unless we were spoken to. Vincent couldn't remember "Bromley," so I told him to just say his first name.

Soon a truck pulled up and right behind it came a white car driven by a lady. She got out and started walking quickly, in her high heels, toward the house. They made a loud clanking noise on the sidewalk.

I couldn't believe my eyes when I saw the large cake she carried. Were we going to eat chocolate cake for breakfast? The lady had big breasts and wore a dark blue dress with small white polka dots on it. The dress had a skinny black patent leather belt that went around her big waist. It isn't nice to call people fat, but she was. She also had on a little round white hat, like she was going to church or something.

Bob opened the door for the lady and gave her a smiling "hello" as he swung his arm toward the inside of the house.

She handed me the cake without saying a word. I couldn't believe how thick the frosting was. Then she waved the two men in the truck to come in. They opened the back of the truck and started bringing in large boxes.

The cake lady smiled at Bob. "My name is Bonnie Jean, and I'm the welcoming committee for the Community First Baptist Church." We had been through a lot of towns, but this was the first time I'd ever heard of a welcoming committee.

Bonnie Jean told the two men to bring in the furniture. In came beds, lamps, a couch, a dining table and chairs, and a TV.

The four of us went crazy. "Wow!" we yelled. "We're getting a TV!" I didn't know why we were getting all these things and didn't care, because this was going to be our last house. I prayed Bob wasn't lying for once.

Bob plugged in the TV, but when we turned it on the picture was fuzzy and you couldn't make out people's faces. Bob said, "I'm going to rig up a set of rabbit ears!"

We looked at each other and giggled. "What is Dad talking about?" I'd seen a rabbit's foot on a key chain, but where did you get rabbit ears. They said a rabbit's foot was good luck, but I'd never understood how cutting off a bunny's foot was good luck; now I worried about a rabbit with no ears.

Bob took a coat hanger from one of the boxes and twisted and turned it in different directions. He put the twisted coat hanger on top of the TV. It was the first time I'd ever heard of a coat hanger called rabbit ears, but they worked! The image on the TV got much clearer. Bob wasn't joking.

Lastly, the men brought in two big boxes marked *male* and *female*. The cake lady said the boxes had clothes for us kids in them. She spoke kind of funny. Bob told us later it was a Southern drawl. I didn't know what he meant by that and wasn't going to ask. The cake lady kept touching Bob's arm and following him around the house. He was touching her arm too. Before Bonnie Jean left, I heard her say, "I'll look for y'all at church tomorrow."

After we ate the whole chocolate cake, it was time to tear open the male and female boxes—that meant boys and girls. Vance and Vincent ignored their box, because they were more interested in the TV with a coat hanger on the top. *Why did that make the TV work?*

Valorie and I brought the female box to our bedroom and took turns claiming pieces. We did this for hours; it was so much fun. My favorite piece was a white blouse with lots of buttons and a small wishing well embroidered on the front pocket. Sewn above the embroidered wishing well were three real gold coins. The coins dangled over the wishing well like they were falling into my pocket. It was the most beautiful blouse I'd ever owned.

---

We got up early the next morning to go to the Baptist church. I asked Bob if it was like going to Mass in the Philippines. No answer. I didn't know why I bothered asking Bob anything.

"It's not called Mass, it's called services," Valorie said, "and Baptists don't have priests, they have preachers."

I took my rosary anyway.

I wore my wishing well blouse and a skirt. The skirt was a little too long, but it didn't matter because it looked great with my new favorite blouse. I figured I had three wishes coming to me—one for each of the coins on my blouse. My first wish was for my mother to come soon, my second wish was not to move anymore, and I thought I'd save my third wish for a rainy day.

We combed our hair and washed our faces, then put on our new used clothes. We even had socks that matched. Vance and Vincent looked clean and handsome. It didn't matter what Bob thought, because I knew I looked beautiful.

When we arrived at church, the cake lady waved wildly at us, reminding me of a girl I once saw drowning in the public pool. The lifeguard saw her waving frantically like that and pulled her out.

Bob warned us one more time, "Make sure to use your new last names while at church."

"Nobody asked our names yesterday," I said. "Why would they today?"

"Don't be stupid Veronica, use your head."

Why did asking questions make me stupid?

The cake lady had saved seats for us up front. The pews looked like the ones in Catholic churches, only shorter; like park benches. The six of us squeezed together onto the short bench. We were used to being crowded together; we usually shared the same bed.

I think the cake lady had saved the pew mostly for Bob. She liked being close to him. She smiled all through the service, and Bob kept patting her hand.

At the end of all the "hallelujahs" and "praise the Lords," the preacher made an announcement.

"Let's welcome Mr. Robert Bromley and his four adopted children," he said.

There was that word I hated: "adopted." I thought it was okay to hate a word but not a person. Everyone started clapping and smiling at us. The cake lady slipped her arm through Bob's arm. I wanted to shout, "We have a mother!" Bob was lying in church! If this was a Catholic church, he'd be sinning.

Using a microphone, the preacher said loudly, "Be good Christians now, and help this poor family." There was the other word I hated: "poor." I got a sick feeling in my stomach, and the more the preacher talked the worse it felt.

Then the preacher started telling everyone about Bob being wounded while in the army. I didn't know that!

"Mr. Bromley adopted these four unfortunate children in his travels through the Orient," he said. "These children were unwanted, and Bob saved them."

I felt like I was going to cry but held my head up like Mom always told me to do. My mother and Soling wanted us more than anything in the world. I don't know why these church people believed Bob; maybe it was because the four of us didn't really look alike. Vincent and I had light brown hair, Vance had dark brown hair, and Valorie had black hair just like Mom.

The ushers started passing collection baskets from the front to the back and the preacher told everyone, "Be generous; dig deep!" A basket got passed in the Catholic church for the poor, too. This church was going to give the whole basket of money to Bob, for the poor Slaughter-Bromley kids.

The service finally ended. I was relieved because my stomach was still hurting, and I needed to get out of there. We walked out of the church with the cake lady holding Bob's arm. The *parishioners* (which sounded like "prisoners" to me) were standing around outside the church, waiting for us. Today

I felt like a prisoner, and I wanted to escape. People came over to shake Bob's hand and pat us on our heads, saying, "You are lucky little children to be able to live in this country with such a loving man." Bob talked to the crowd gathering around him.

The cake lady looked like she wasn't going to let any of the other church ladies get too close to Bob. She offered out loud, "I'd be delighted to cook Sunday dinner for y'all."

I loved the idea, and Bob must have too because he said, "Thank you Bonnie Jean, I look forward to seeing you."

She smiled a really big smile when Bob said that.

Two women walked up to Vincent and asked his name. Vincent just looked up at me, so I answered for him, "His name is Vincent, and he's a little shy." I was glad no one asked my name because I didn't like lying. I just wanted to go back to the house.

While we were standing by the truck waiting for Bob, a group of girls my age came over. I stood up tall, pushing out my chest to make sure they saw the wishing well on my blouse. One of the girls started laughing and said, "I told you that was my blouse. Don't you recognize it? I threw it in the donation box for this poor family." They walked away without even saying good-bye.

At that moment, I knew what my third wish was: not to be poor anymore.

We weren't in Georgia long. Bob lied again.

## Chapter 29:

# BINGO!

Bob held up a five hundred–dollar bill. He said it was five hundred one-dollar bills put together. That was a lot of money to be in one piece of paper! I asked him where he got it, and he said, "A windfall."

I never knew where Bob got his money. It seemed he had either plenty or he didn't have a dime to his name. I knew wind didn't just blow money into your hands, although I had found a dollar once when we were at a laundromat. I looked around to see if it belonged to someone, but we were the only ones in there. That was lucky for us, because Valorie and I had to wash three bags of clothes. We had enough nickels to use the washers and dryers but not enough to buy soap. I figured if we used hot water, we wouldn't need soap, but that found dollar bought four small boxes of Tide from the soap machine.

Bob said we were going to spend the five hundred–dollar bill at the Jack Tar Hotel, and we needed to buy fancy new clothes.

I was tired of wondering where we were going or what we were doing, so I just did what I was told; life was easier that way. I was eleven years old now, and I'd stopped asking questions and put all my faith and trust in God. Sooner or later, God would get to us. There were people in the world that were poorer and needed him more. I'd be patient; He would get to us soon. I knew it in my heart.

We went shopping at a store called I. Magnin. To my surprise, Bob wanted to pick out our clothes. Valorie and I ended up with matching pink ruffled dresses with matching ruffled socks, white shiny shoes, and white gloves. I had never owned a pair of gloves like these before. I wasn't sure what they were for. They weren't the kind you'd wear to play in the snow or work on a farm. I was sure these gloves would get dirty in an instant, but I wasn't going to tell Bob that. Vance and Vincent both got suits with white shirts and red bow ties. They looked handsome, and I looked like a stupid doll. I was old enough to pick my own clothes. I hated pink and definitely wouldn't have picked white patent leather shoes.

The next day, we drove to the Jack Tar Hotel in San Francisco. Bob said it was a classy place. When we pulled up to the front of the hotel, a man came out and opened the car door, held his hand out, and called me Mademoiselle. I told him my name was Veronica, not Mad-whatever, and I grabbed Vincent's hand instead of his because I didn't know him. The man smiled and stepped aside so Vincent and I could get out. I thanked him for closing the car door.

Why was he doing all that? I wasn't old, I could open and close my own door. And he had white gloves on too. Why? I'd never seen a place like this before. All the people looked rich, like the people at I. Magnin. Where was Bob getting all this money?

Bob was wearing a new white shirt, a gray jacket, and black pants. His hair was perfect, and his face was as smooth as a baby's bottom. That's what Bob always said after he shaved. I knew a baby's bottom didn't feel like Bob's face. Vincent's bottom had been much smoother when he was a baby.

We walked through two huge glass doors opened by two men who also wore white gloves. It's like they didn't want us touching anything. I finally figured out that the gloves were part of their uniform, because everyone was wearing the same thing.

Bob smiled and handed money to all the men opening and closing doors. *What for?* He asked one of them where the bar was. They pointed to a place that looked like a fancy restaurant. We walked in and sat at a small glass table circled by a white leather couch. It was like a picture from a magazine.

A beautiful waitress came up, smiled, and said her name was Alexandria. She seemed different from most other waitresses I'd seen. I didn't know why, but she seemed nicer and politer. She asked Bob what his pleasure was, which I supposed meant what would make him feel good. Bob said Scotch on the rocks. Then Alexandria turned to Valorie and me.

"And what would your pleasure be?" she asked.

"We're too young to drink," I said.

She laughed, said she would bring us something special, and winked. I liked it when she did that. It made me feel like we were friends.

"Do you like cherries?" she asked.

"Yes!" I nodded.

She looked at Bob and said she was going to bring Shirley Temples for the girls and Roy Rogers for the boys.

Bob winked at her and said, "Sure." His wink and her wink didn't feel the same. I loved Shirley Temple and Roy Rogers. Why did our drinks have their names? I wasn't going to ask, I wanted to let it be a surprise.

Alexandria came back with glasses that were hard to hold. Bob said they were martini glasses. Valorie's and my martinis were pink with red cherries, and the boys' martinis were yellow with green cherries. I had never seen a green cherry before.

Bob held up his glass and said, "Let's toast."

We carefully lifted our glasses and clinked them together. Vincent spilled a little, but Bob didn't say anything.

Our martinis were delicious. I wanted to ask why Alexandria called martinis Shirley Temple and Roy Rogers, but I knew what the answer would be so I didn't bother.

Alexandria took our pictures with Bob's camera. First Bob had a picture with the boys, then he took one with Valorie and me. Alexandria told us there was something going on in the main ballroom and it might be fun for us to drop in, because there were lots of prizes being given away. Bob told Alexandria he was waiting for a friend.

*What friend?* I wondered.

Just then, a lady came walking in. She walked right up to our table wearing a really tight dress. Bob said it fit her like a glove. Her dress was red and white with a short little jacket. She was wearing red high heels and carried a small red purse. She reminded me of the wicked witch in *The Wizard of Oz* because she had a mean face.

Bob stood up and said, "Rita, you're late," and then he hugged and kissed her. As he introduced each of us to her, she glanced at us with her mean face, then hugged Bob again.

Rita said she wanted to take us to the fund-raiser she

was holding. I'd never heard the word fund-raiser before and knew not to ask. We followed Bob and Rita into a giant room where a party was going on. Alexandria was right! All the tables had pretty tablecloths with fresh flowers in the middle. Music was playing, and a man in the front was trying to talk to everyone over a microphone. It was really noisy. I was having fun already!

Rita found a table with six seats.

"Who is this party for?" I asked Bob.

"Wait and see," he said.

I wanted to shout, "Answer my question, just once!"

Rita came back to the table with a stack of Bingo cards. She gave each of us two cards. There was a glass bowl on the table filled with colored glass rocks. I knew how to play Bingo, and I realized the rocks were for covering the numbers on our cards. I'd played Bingo at a church in Mississippi once but hadn't won anything. I told Vincent I would help him with his cards because he had never played before.

The man at the front of the room finally got everyone's attention. Now I was excited! I had a feeling this was going to be my lucky day.

Rita went to the front of the room and talked over the microphone for a while. She said something about raising money for underprivileged children. I knew what that meant, it meant poor children. I'd heard it many times before. Did Rita know we were poor? She couldn't, because we had new clothes and Bob had a five hundred–dollar bill.

I watched as a man up front started twirling the Bingo balls in a big metal basket. When he stopped, Rita reached in and pulled out a ball and then handed it to the man, and he called out the number.

The first three numbers were on mine and Vincent's

cards. I was sure we were going to win something, but just then, from across the room, someone yelled, "Bingo!" It was an old man and he won a set of kitchen knives. I guess they were special knives, because he was so happy.

We cleared our cards and put our glass rocks back in the bowl. Bob gave his cards to Vance and Vincent. We had to win now. Vincent was holding a handful of glass rocks, getting ready to put them where I pointed. Bob got up and walked to the back of the room to talk with a group of men. *I guess he doesn't want to play Bingo anymore*, I thought.

Then the man in the front took another ball from Rita's hand and yelled, "B4!"

I froze. I had covered all my numbers across.

Again, the man said, "B4!"

"Bingo! Bingo!" I jumped out of my chair and held up my card; then I realized everyone was looking at me and quickly sat down.

"Come up here, sweetheart," the man at the front of the room said. "Show me your card."

Everyone started clapping. Instead of thinking I was ugly or poor, they were thinking I was a winner. I looked back at Bob, and he motioned for me to go up front. I was so nervous.

When I got up front, the man looked at my card for a minute and then said, "Congratulations beautiful, you have won the best deep-sea fishing pole and reel ever made." He smiled. "Do you know how to fish?"

"Doesn't everyone?" I said.

The people in the audience laughed, and I felt my face get warm. The man asked me how old I was, and I told him.

"How does a sweet little girl like you know how to fish?" he asked.

"My father taught me," I said.

He handed me the beautiful dark blue fishing pole. I was so proud. I loved the shiny new fishing pole, even though it was heavier than any pole I had ever held; that just meant I could catch the biggest fish now. I started to leave the stage.

"What kind of fish have you caught?" the man asked before I left.

I nervously rattled off every fish I had ever reeled in: flounder, tuna, perch, snapper, mullet, and catfish.

He looked surprised and patted me on the head. "Not only is this little girl pretty, she is one heck of a fisherman."

My face felt hot again and I mumbled, "Fishergirl."

I couldn't have smiled any bigger as I walked back to my seat with my prize. The people in the room were still clapping.

Bob came over and asked to see my fishing pole and took it from me. He looked it over carefully and said, "This is a very expensive deep-sea fishing pole. I'll take it to the car for safekeeping."

"I'll keep it with me," I said. "No one will take it."

I only got to hold my new fishing pole for a couple of minutes before I had to give it to Bob. I wasn't feeling happy anymore and was finished playing Bingo. Bob told me to go thank Rita for the Bingo cards. I did as I was told and when I got back, my prize was gone.

I never saw my fishing pole again.

## Chapter 30:

# GIGOLO

We'd been driving for hours. Valorie read her dictionary out loud to give us something to do. We called her the walking dictionary because there wasn't any word she didn't know, and if there was, she'd reach for the pocket dictionary she always kept in her pocket. Valorie was on the G's in her dictionary when she came to the word *gigolo*. Most of the time she would pick a word she wasn't sure about or one she thought we didn't know.

I asked Valorie to read the definition. She said, "*Gigolo*. A man supported financially by an older woman, one who lavishes him with gifts like expensive clothes and cars."

"What does 'financially' mean?" I asked.

"It means when a woman gives a man money," she said, and then she told me what "lavished" meant without me even asking.

I couldn't believe it! That was our father! Most of the ladies Bob took out were older than him, not counting Esther in Mississippi or the lady with lots of makeup, Rosalina, at the Hi Ho Inn. Anna May, the cake lady, Bonnie Jean, and Rita were just a few of the older women Bob had gone out with. All of them lavished Bob with lots of nice things without him asking.

Sally Doll was different. She didn't like Bob as much as the older women did, and I think that made Bob mad. I know Sally wouldn't let Bob gigolo her because she had lots of boyfriends at her work that gave her money. Bob had tried to get money from Sally by selling me as collateral; when she gave me back, he'd promised to pay her back, but I wasn't sure if he ever had, so maybe he had gigoloed her.

Valorie read another G word: "*Goddess*. A woman who is adored, especially for her beauty."

That was my mother! The customers at our coffee shop thought she was a goddess too. She was beautiful and adored by everyone. And she wasn't an older woman; she was younger than Bob.

By the time all those older women found out Bob was a gigolo, we were gone. Now I understood why we always left in the middle of the night without saying good-bye to anyone. Bob was cheating them, and that's why we had lots of money sometimes and other times had none. Finding an older woman was like finding a job. I wondered if all those times Bob went looking for "work," he was really looking for an older woman to gigolo. I guessed all the kissing and hugging was fake, because we always left as soon as he got enough money. I didn't think he liked working because he never stayed long at his jobs as a car salesman or an insurance agent. Finding older women to gigolo was easier than regular jobs, and he made more money. All Bob had to do was kiss and hug them, and they fell in love with him.

I started thinking about Anna May in Texas. She was the nicest older woman, and I wished Bob had really loved her; I had, even though Fleas had been murdered on her farm. I bet after she got the money for her farm and gave it to Bob, she thought they would get married. Bob was supposed to open a used car lot and make enough money so she wouldn't have to work, but instead, we left. Anna May must have been surprised and sad when she found out she didn't have Bob, us, or her money. I wondered if being a gigolo was stealing.

In Georgia, the cake lady, Bonnie Jean, and Bob had seemed to love each other a lot. I'd known not to get close to Bonnie Jean, though, because the ladies Bob loved never seemed to work out. Bonnie had liked us a little but spent most of her time holding on to Bob.

One Saturday night, Bonnie Jean was cooking collard greens with bacon and fried chicken at our house. She wouldn't let us eat till Bob got home. When he finally did, it was really late, and Bonnie Jean was mad. As soon as Bob walked through the front door, drunk, they got in a big fight.

Us kids moved to our room when the yelling started. Bonnie Jean was shouting about how he'd cheated her or cheated on her. I'm not sure which one; it could have been both. Before she left, slamming the door behind her, with the food still on the stove, she said something about reporting him and wanting her down payment back. I asked Valorie what that was all about and she said it had something to do with money. We left in the middle of the night with whatever fit into our new car. Greensboro didn't turn out to be our forever home like Bob promised after all.

The last woman we lived with was Rita, from the Jack Tar Hotel. She was the only older woman who didn't like us kids even a little bit. She loved Bob, but I heard her tell him they should send us away to boarding school before they got married. I'd run away before going to another St. Clara's; we all would. I'd told Bob to leave us with Uncle Ted and Auntie Feling, since we were in California, or even Grandma Phyllis in Colorado, but he said that wouldn't be necessary. I wondered what he was going to do with us, and worried we'd end up being sent away. I started being extra nice to Rita and her daughter, Carolyn, hoping they wouldn't get rid of us.

Carolyn was much older than me and mean, like Tommy. She was never home and didn't talk to us when she was. I don't think she liked Bob either. I hated staying at Rita's house, even though it was a rich person's house. Just when I started to really worry about what they were going to do with us, we left in Rita's Mercedes early in the morning. It was the most beautiful car I had ever been in.

We didn't drive for long, because Bob traded the Mercedes for another car. He told me the man at the car lot was going to bring it back to Rita. I was glad he didn't gigolo Rita for her car, even though I didn't like her. That's how we ended up with the car we were in, which smelled like cigarettes and didn't have a radio.

Valorie read another new word on our drive: "*Gracious*. Courteous, kind, polite; showing grace." Now that was a wonderful word.

"That's what I want to be," I told Valorie, "because everyone will love me and want to be my friend."

Bob was a gigolo, Mom was a goddess, I was gracious. Vincent said he want to be the monster Godzilla from a comic he had seen. Vance chimed in and said he wanted to be GI Joe. I asked Valorie to pick a G word. She thought about it and said she wanted to be a genius because they were highly intellectual or smart. Valorie was smart, so I figured she was already a genius. I liked playing the dictionary game.

Bob got off the freeway to get gas again and said, "This damn car is a pig on gas."

As usual, I had no idea what he meant.

"It's costing me a fortune just to get back to Los Angeles," he grumbled.

That was the best news! This meant we'd see our auntie and uncle, who we'd only seen a couple of times since we first got here. I'd ask if they'd heard anything from the Philippines or about Mom. They would tell me the truth about Mom and Soling.

Bob would need to look for a job when we got to Los Angeles, which meant we could hopefully stay with our auntie and uncle, like we had the last time. I wondered if his new job would be an older woman. It seemed like men lied and stole from lonely women who just wanted to get married and have someone to love them.

I was going to grow up to be gracious, have my own business, and be honest. I wasn't going to steal or lie to people, and I wouldn't need a man to love me, except maybe Vance and Vincent when they grew up.

I was a warrior, and no one was going to gigolo me.

## Chapter 31:

# AN ANGEL IN THE ROOM

Once we got to Los Angeles, we went to see our aunt and uncle. Just like I thought, Bob wanted to borrow money to get us into a new apartment. Before we arrived at their house, Bob ordered us not to bring up anything about Mom. When I asked why I got the usual, "Just do what I say, or you'll stay in the car."

It had been a long time since we'd seen our aunt and uncle. I had so many questions for them but knew better than to cross our father.

Auntie didn't mention Mom; that was a good sign, because if anything bad had happened to her, they would have heard about it. She asked where we had been and how come I'd never called. I told her I'd tried but her phone didn't work anymore.

My aunt made a funny face, then said, "What? Our number is working! Maybe you dialed the wrong number!"

I told her I knew it by heart, DU-1-2409.

Meanwhile, Bob was talking to Uncle Ted, saying, "I know it's a lot of money, Ted, but you'll get it back in spades, I promise. I'll have it back to you in two weeks." Why would my uncle want spades instead of money? I wanted to tell Uncle Ted not to trust our father, because he never kept his promises.

We didn't stay long, but Bob said we'd be back in a couple of weeks. I was glad. I'd wait till then to find a way to ask my aunt about Mom. She'd tell me the truth.

⁂

The apartment Bob found was in Glendale, California. It wasn't really an apartment, it was a two-car garage made into a place for a teenage boy, like Tommy, to live. But the teenage boy had moved out and his father, Bob's new friend, was letting us live there until Bob found a job—again.

The garage-apartment had a small bathroom, a kitchen that was hardly usable, and our bedroom, which was a space separated by a bed sheet hanging from the ceiling. The floor was cold concrete, and the only heat came from two small electric heaters, one in our room and one in the living area.

It was a few days before Christmas in 1963 when Bob received a late-night phone call. We were getting ready for bed when we heard him talking angrily to whoever was on the other end. He started yelling, "No, I'm not going to do that, and she can't threaten me!" He was getting angrier by the moment.

I motioned for everyone to move to the bedroom. I told the boys to be quiet and get into bed but to keep their clothes on in case we had to leave. We kept quiet, waiting for Bob to calm down.

We had been living with our father for almost four years and knew what to do and what not to do when it came to his temper. Our choices were to go to our room or leave the house completely. This sounded like a go-to-our-room situation, at least for now.

When Bob hung up the phone, he started walking back and forth, mumbling under his breath. If things got worse, I'd have to put warm clothes on the boys and all of us would leave the garage. Usually, when Bob was angry, the four of us would get dressed and walk around the block until he left, fell asleep, or came to find us. I hoped it wouldn't get to that, because it was cold out.

Why was he upset? Whatever it was, Bob wasn't telling us. I didn't think anyone should be mad at Christmas, it was the most special time of the year.

Suddenly, it got quiet on the other side of the sheet, so I peeked around. Bob was going through a stack of papers, but when he couldn't find what he was looking for, he started slamming drawers and stomping around again. Then, without warning, he whipped the sheet aside.

"Put clean clothes on," he snapped.

I wanted to ask him where we were going but didn't. I just started to pack our things.

"Stop packing," he said. "We're coming back. We're just going to your aunt and uncle's house."

That was the most terrific news. I stopped worrying and started feeling excited instead.

We didn't have much to choose from when it came to our clothes, and tonight most of what we owned was in the laundry. Bob didn't have the money to take us to the laundromat, so I washed our underwear in the sink. Having only a few possessions made it easier to pack and leave in a hurry. The laundromat had ruined the pink ruffled dresses that Valorie and I had worn to the Jack Tar Hotel. I was glad, because I wasn't going to wear mine again anyway.

We quickly looked for our cleanest clothes. The boys put on their jeans with flannel shirts that probably needed washing, I wore my plaid skirt with my trusty white blouse and my only sweater, and Valorie wore her white blouse with a navy skirt and a jacket that we both shared. The boys combed their hair, and Valorie pulled my hair into a tight ponytail. I wished I had washed my hair, but at least in a ponytail, you couldn't tell it needed washing.

Once we were dressed, we waited eagerly for Bob. It was about 10:00 p.m. but we weren't tired even a little bit.

Bob was still searching for something. His hands were shaking, and he seemed nervous. Finally, he found our passports and put them in his shirt pocket. I wondered what that meant and hoped he wasn't taking us somewhere far. Were we really going to Auntie Feling and Uncle Ted's house? Was he lying?

*Please God*, I prayed silently, *let us be going to our aunt and uncle's house, and please let us stay there*.

I hoped this Christmas was going to be different than the previous Christmas, which we'd spent on the road. None of us had even remembered it was Christmas last year.

In the Philippines, we would start getting ready for Christmas right after the Feast Day of Saint Jude on October 28, my birthday. I remembered all the food preparations and how beautifully decorated the church was. Jesus's birthday was a special time of the year, like Easter, only we didn't have to go to church every day. The whole family would be together on these special days. We'd sing and dance to music that my cousins played on the piano or guitar. No one yelled or got mad at anybody. Everyone was happy on Jesus's birthday.

I wondered why Bob was taking us to Auntie Feling and Uncle Ted's house so late. We only ever visited them in the daytime unless we were spending the night, and he hadn't let us do that since we'd been back in Los Angeles. I was pretty sure he'd given up being a gigolo, because he never shaved or combed his hair perfect anymore. I didn't think the women liked it when he dragged the four of us along everywhere they went.

If tonight had something to do with Christmas, why would he be mad? I'd stopped trying to figure out why Bob did what he did long ago, but I still prayed that this was going to be a good night. My Uncle Ted and Auntie Feling might have Christmas presents for us. They spoiled us with all kinds of gifts when we stayed with them, probably because they had no children and loved us.

Once, they took us to a Filipino restaurant near downtown Los Angeles called the Nipa Hut. Most everyone was Filipino and spoke our language. I didn't understand as much as I had when I was younger, but I'd liked being there, because it reminded me of our happy life in Cebu with Mom.

It was getting harder and harder to remember our coffee shop. What did Soling look like? Was her hair short or long? I tried to picture our apartment above the coffee shop and wondered what color my blanket was. I never wanted to forget my mother or the Philippines. I was glad we were going to see our auntie and uncle, because I wanted to ask them about our mother and if they'd heard from her. In order for Mom to find us, we had to stay in one place: my auntie's house.

In the past four years, we'd lived in six states and gone to seven schools. I was tired of moving. I wished Bob would just leave us with our auntie and uncle permanently. My grandma

Phyllis had told him three years ago to stop dragging us all over the country, but he didn't listen to anyone. I missed my grandma Phyllis and wanted to wish her a Merry Christmas. I'd ask Auntie Feling if we could call her. I knew they had each other's phone numbers because Auntie Feling had told me she knew my grandma. And if she'd forgotten, she could ask the operator to look up her number in Colorado.

Bob lit a cigarette and told us to get into the car. We didn't say a word for fear he would change his mind. It was cold outside, so we quickly piled into the backseat of our beat-up car, which was always low on gas. I hoped we had enough to get to Los Angeles.

No one wanted to sit in the front with Bob because he was in a bad mood. I was beginning to worry about where we were really going. He had put our passports in his pocket. I didn't want Vincent to worry too, so I whispered in his ear, "I think we may be getting presents."

His eyes got really big, and he covered his mouth with both hands to keep from shouting. "Do you think we'll get more than one present?" he whispered back.

I frowned at him. "Don't be greedy, it's Christmas!"

I told Vincent I wanted a bike for Christmas but knew if we moved, I wouldn't be able to take it with us, so I hoped for a new jacket with a fur collar instead. Vincent wanted a slinky or a super ball. Vance wanted the GI Jo action figure instead of more little green army men. Valorie wanted a new diary with a lock and key.

*A book that locks. Why would anyone want that?* I wondered.

We drove in silence all the way to Los Angeles while Bob smoked his Salem cigarettes one after another. We squeezed each other's hands with excitement as we got closer. I was sure we'd get at least one present, and maybe even two.

When we got off the freeway, I was relieved to see that I recognized the streets going to our aunt and uncle's house.

It was late when we turned on Vendome Street. I wanted to start clapping but didn't dare to move. I couldn't wait to get into the house. It was cold, and Auntie Feling and Uncle Ted would make us warm and feed us.

We pulled up in front of their house. The roof of the house was outlined in colorful Christmas lights. I wanted to cry, it was so beautiful. This was what I'd been hoping for: Christmas decorations and a Christmas tree.

All the lights in the house were on. I was happy but surprised they were still awake. My uncle and auntie were pretty old and usually went to bed early. I thought there must be something special going on for them to stay up until almost midnight. I was getting excited again and my stomach felt like it was flipping around, but not in a bad way.

Before getting out of the car, Bob turned around and looked at us with a mean face. "We are not staying long. Do you understand!?"

What? I wanted to stay overnight. It was almost midnight! But you never argued with Bob, you just said, "Yes sir." I was still happy to be there and hoped Auntie could talk Bob into letting us stay with them since it was our Christmas break.

Vance was the first one out of the car, running to ring the doorbell before Vincent. It was always a race for the doorbell. I told Vincent to remember his manners, even though I knew he would. He had just turned seven and didn't need much reminding.

As we stood in front of the house, waiting for someone to answer the door, we started fidgeting and stamping our feet. It was cold, but I was more nervous than cold.

Finally, Auntie Feling opened the door to the glass-enclosed porch. Her eyes were red and watery, like she had been crying. Oh no! I hoped I wasn't wrong about tonight. Had something happened to our mother? To Uncle Ted?

Auntie didn't say anything as she bent down to give each of us a big hug before we stepped onto the porch. Her hug was a lot harder than her usual hugs.

"Is everything okay?" I asked, feeling panicked inside.

She smiled really big. "Yes, everything is wonderful."

"Do we get presents?" Vincent blurted out.

"Yes! The best present!" Auntie said.

I was relieved. She wouldn't be smiling if something bad had happened to Mom or Uncle Ted. Bob stayed behind on the sidewalk and didn't even say hello. Auntie Feling took Valorie's hand, and then mine, and led us from the porch to the large wooden front door. As my aunt slowly pushed the heavy door open, I was the first one to step in.

I stepped into their huge living room, looked up, and suddenly felt light-headed. I thought I was dreaming. My heart started to pound—not because of the big Christmas tree with all its ornaments but because of the beautiful angel sitting on the couch in a knee-length, sky blue skirt and white blouse. She wore pearls around her neck with matching earrings. The angel had short, wavy black hair, her skin was creamy, and her red lips were perfect. She had an angel's smile and dark eyes that sparkled. The beautiful angel was sitting sideways on the couch with her ankles crossed and her hands clasped lightly on her lap. She sat tall, her face glowing like there was a light shining on it.

I couldn't believe my eyes. I blinked several times and then ran to the angel. She hugged me tight, and I hugged her back twice as hard, promising to never let her go.

The angel's name was Mommy.

An Angel in the Room Happiest Day of My Life, 1963

## Chapter 32:

# DIED AND GONE TO HEAVEN

From that moment on, I swore, I'd never leave my mother's side again. We were all happy to see this beautiful woman, but for me it was much, much more. It was a dream come true, the answer to my many prayers. I was rescued. I'd known God would hear me. My life now had meaning. I no longer had to feel fear daily or pray my rosary nightly, hoping our mother would come for us. There was no more crying and wondering if Mom was dead or alive. She was here. I could touch her whenever I wanted. My job as Vincent and Vance's mother and protector had come to an end. I would no longer have to figure out what kind of mood Bob was in or if my name was Bromley or Slaughter. That bad feeling in my stomach would finally go away. Seeing my mother for the first time in four years, I felt like I had died and gone to Heaven.

I looked down and saw Vincent hanging on to me. I had my head on Mom's lap, and both my arms were wrapped around her waist; I was holding on to her the way that Vincent held on to me when he felt scared. I was soaking up the warmth of her body, the familiar smell of her skin, the softness of her touch. The more I touched her the more real she became.

Mom spoke calmly to Vincent as she put her beautiful hand with her long fingers on his cheek. "Ting Ting," she said. "Do you know who I am?"

Ting Ting had been Vincent's nickname in the Philippines; I remembered as soon as Mom said it.

Vincent got close to my ear. "Who is this lady, Mommy?"

I felt a combination of anger and sadness. I pressed Vincent away from me and told him, "She is your real mother!"

Vincent had a puzzled look on his face; then, to my surprise, he moved in close and hugged Mom around her neck. I wished I knew what Vincent was thinking just then. He seemed to understand as he remembered her for the first time since he was three.

Valorie had lots of questions for Mom. I wanted to tell Val, "I told you Mom was coming," but I noticed Val didn't look surprised to see Mom; maybe she had believed me after all. Valorie walked over and hugged our mother, then sat down on the couch next to her. Mom held Valorie's hand as Val asked her questions. Her other hand stroked my hair as I continued to lie on her lap. Valorie wanted to know how our Filipino grandfather was, if we were going back to the Philippines, if we had to leave our father and live with her. It was one question after another.

Mom spoke softly when answering Valorie, without yelling or making anyone feel stupid. Val loved our father more than I did—a lot more. She worried that if our father left, we wouldn't see him anymore. Didn't Valorie understand that Mom wasn't Bob? That she'd never make us do anything we didn't want to?

"It's okay, Valorie, if you want to go with your father tonight," Mom said. "I'll see you tomorrow." She saw Valorie's attachment to Bob and reassured her by saying, "Don't worry, my darling, everything is going to be alright."

I loved those words.

Vance sat close to Uncle Ted and stared at Mom. When Valorie was done asking her questions, Mom reached her hand out to Vance. He looked scared as he stood and slowly walked toward her; Uncle Ted encouraged him by placing his hand on his back.

Vance waited a second, then said, "I thought you were dead. Dad said your plane crashed and you went to Heaven." After a long pause, he said, "Are you really our mother?"

With a look of sadness, Mom reached both her arms toward Vance. He moved quickly toward her and gave her a long hug. She kissed his head several times before he stood up and went back to sit next to Uncle Ted again. Vance was a sensitive boy, and I could tell he was confused. He looked lost. I felt sorry for him.

It was way past midnight now and everyone was trying to figure out what to do next. On the porch, Bob was talking loudly to our aunt. Everything was happening so fast; my heart was pounding. I felt excitement and fear all at the same time. Mom was the only calm person in the room, speaking with a soft, loving voice. I was her child, her *babae*, her baby, her little girl.

When Bob came inside and talked to Mom, he used his angry voice, but she answered politely. She was the opposite of Bob. You never knew what to expect from him but always knew what to expect from her: kindness, courtesy, and graciousness.

That night, Vance and Valorie went home with Bob. At first, he demanded that we all go with him until he got things "sorted out," whatever that meant. But I would never trust him again and didn't want Mom to either. I knew in my stomach not to go with him; I feared he wouldn't bring me back. He would have to drag me away if he wanted me to leave—and he almost did. He grabbed my ponytail and tried to pull me off my mother. But I held on to her like it was a matter of life or death, which it was for me. I couldn't and wouldn't live another day without her.

Vincent started to cry and held on to me as Bob pulled. Mom stood up, put her hand up to Bob, and said, "Stop!" I knew she wasn't going to let Bob hurt us. "I'll keep Veronica and Vincent for tonight," she said, "and Vance and Valorie can go with you if they want to, as long as you have them back in the morning." She told Bob not to make it harder than it needed to be, because the law was on her side.

For whatever reason, Valorie and Vance didn't seem to mind going back with Bob. Mom hugged and kissed them and told them she'd see them in the morning. I wondered if Mom was doing the right thing after what happened at the coffee shop four years ago.

"Don't worry," she told me. "He's going to bring them back; everything is going to be alright."

I trusted Mom. I knew she would make sure Valorie and Vance came back. Auntie Feling told them we'd have a family party with lots of our favorite foods, and that we'd open Christmas presents. I saw Vance's eyes get big, and his smile get bigger. Uncle Ted was the best at making Filipino food, especially *pancit*, which Filipinos made for good luck. I hoped Mom would make her donuts, because now that I was twelve, I could help her.

Mom handed Bob some papers and said, "Be here in the morning, and I won't press charges." She looked serious but not mad. She was strong. She was a warrior. The papers seemed to be proof that we belonged to her.

Bob grabbed the papers and headed for the door without a word. Valorie was right behind him. Vance waved and then followed Valorie. I could tell Vance wanted to stay but was still unsure. He stuck close to Valorie like Vincent did to me.

Mom was in charge now. I no longer had to be a grown-up.

I talked nonstop to Mom until I couldn't keep my eyes open. She listened patiently and answered all my questions. She held Vincent and me until it was time for bed, and then the three of us slept together in the guest room. Auntie Feling said we'd have plenty of room because it was a king-size bed. I thought it should be called a queen's bed.

Vincent slept on one side of Mom and I slept on the other. I didn't sleep much that night. I kept waking up to make sure Mom was still there; each time, she was.

---

Valorie and Vance came back the next morning, just like Mom had said they would. Bob dropped them off with our clothes in the big green duffel bag from the army surplus store. I ran out to see if he'd brought my secret box. Vance had it in his hands. I hugged him for remembering to bring it. Bob left without saying good-bye to anyone in the house.

Vance looked happy to be back but Valorie still seemed concerned, especially as Bob drove away. She wanted to know when he was coming back. Mom told Val she could see him whenever she liked. Valorie seemed satisfied with Mom's answer. Mom wasn't a liar; she would keep her promises. She wasn't Bob.

For the first time in four years, we were together as a family, just like I remembered it. My memories of living above our coffee shop came rushing back. I remembered the color of my bedspread, the eight stools downstairs at the counter, and the souvenirs that hung on the coffee shop door, twinkling in the sunlight. I felt loved and protected again. No one was ever going to hurt us now that Mom had come.

Valorie was thirteen, I was twelve, Vance was ten, and Vincent had just turned seven. Mom told Vincent she was going to get him a belated birthday present.

"I turned seven on December 4th," Vincent said proudly.

Mom tilted her head and said, "Your birthday was a week ago, December 17th."

We were all surprised by this. The rest of us told her our birthdays, and found out we were wrong about Vance's, too: his wasn't January 1st, it was January 11th. Vance was happy to know his birthday was coming, and he'd get another present. Valorie and I had our birthdays correct. Once, Bob had tried to convince me my birthday was October 31st, on Halloween, but I knew I was born on the Feast Day of Saint Jude and that was October 28th.

Mom hugged and kissed us all morning. "You've all grown so much," she said, "and I've missed so many birthdays." I could tell she wanted to cry as much as I did, but I knew she stayed strong for us.

She was really here! My nightmare was over.

## Chapter 33:

# OUT OF SIGHT, OUT OF MIND

I didn't ask about Bob after that first night. I didn't hate my father but didn't love him either. The little love I'd had for him had ended at St. Clara's. It had ended when he sold me to Sally Doll. It had ended in Brownsville at the fish camp. It had ended with every promise he hadn't kept. It had ended when he said Mom was dead. In my mind, he no longer was part of my life.

Valorie, on the other hand, missed our father. She wanted to spend time with him. Mom explained that school came first, but she could visit with him on the weekends. Valorie felt our father needed her; he always called her his *big girl* and told her how much he counted on her.

I reminded Val of all the times we were hungry, how he wasn't around when she almost died from the catfish. I reminded her that he'd taken us from Mom, and how hard it had been going to so many schools and living in our truck. Most important, I reminded her that he'd lied about the plane crash.

Val didn't seem to care about any of it. Her answer was always the same: "He's our father, and he was only trying to protect us."

Protect us from what?

"You don't know the whole story, Veronica," she'd say. "He was doing the best he could." Valorie hung on every word my father said, but I didn't believe a word of what he said. How could she love him, and why didn't she see him for what he really was—a liar, a gigolo, a stealer? Worst of all, he had stolen us from Mom.

Vance and Vincent didn't seem to mind either way. They were just happy to live in one place, sleep in the same bed every night, and have one person to call Mommy.

I think having Mom was what Vance liked the best. Every time he'd gotten close to one of the women Bob was dating, he'd woken up one day to find her gone. I'd been Vincent's mommy, so as long as he had me, he'd felt safe. Bob had called Valorie "the woman of the house," so she hadn't needed a mother.

I told Mom I'd never believed Bob's story of the plane crash—that I'd known in my heart that she and Soling were alive. "I knew God would bring you back because He showed me in a dream," I said. "I was patient and prayed like you taught me."

Mom had tears running down her face as I talked about how hard it was being a mommy to Vincent and the many times I cried for her. She said how sorry she was for everything. "What happened to you was all my fault," she said, and now she was crying with her hands covering her face. She kept repeating, "I should have known. Soling was right. I should have known."

I told Mom not to cry because God answered our prayers and brought us back together. Then I started crying, but not for the same reason Mom was. I was crying because I was happy being her *babae* again.

I asked about Soling. I wanted to know why she didn't come with her. Soling went everywhere with my mother. Mom said Soling was getting old and petitioning her would take a long time. Soling needed a passport too. But she missed me and hoped we'd go back to the Philippines soon. I asked about Lolo and Lola and all our cousins. I asked about the coffee shop and who was taking care of it. Mom said everyone was fine, and they were glad we had found each other. The whole family prayed every day for our safe return. Mom had sold Lee's Coffee Shop and it was now a souvenir shop where they served Sanka and Filipino pastries.

Auntie Feling told me that Mom had a nervous breakdown after our father took us. She said a letter had come from Mom's sister Sofia telling her that Mom was in a hospital. It was a special hospital for people whose minds were all mixed up. When someone was so sad that they couldn't go to work or even leave their house, they went there. Auntie had never told us about the letter because she was secretly trying to help Mom come to America.

Even though Bob had caused Mom to have a nervous breakdown, she never said anything bad about him. "If you can't say something nice about a person," she'd always taught us, "don't say anything at all." So she didn't say anything about Bob.

Mom was fighting for full custody of us, which meant we wouldn't have to live with Bob ever again. She'd told Bob she wouldn't press charges for kidnapping us from the Philippines if he let us stay with her 'til the court's ruling.

I understood most of what Mom was talking about but not the court part. We were Mom's children, so why did she have to fight for us?

In the end, there was no fight, because Bob left town. He didn't fight for us. He didn't really want us. I knew he didn't love us either. I think he was relieved to not be taking care of us anymore. I also think he realized that Mom wouldn't quit fighting 'til she won. She was a warrior.

## Chapter 34:

# LIFE AFTER BOB

The next few weeks were spent catching up and apartment hunting. Mom went through the *Los Angeles Times* looking for a place to live and a job. In the meantime, it was fun being at my aunt and uncle's house. They told us to stay as long as we wanted because there was lots of room. We cooked, cleaned, and shopped together. We had a schedule for eating breakfast, lunch, and dinner. We sat together for meals, and Mom led a prayer before anyone took a bite.

Mom was happy to see we remembered our manners. I told her how I'd taught Vincent and Vance everything she'd taught me, like how to pray and to be kind, grateful, and polite. Mom was proud of me.

Mom gave each of us daily chores, just like we'd had at the coffee shop. It was fun making our beds, doing laundry, and helping in the kitchen. We told her how we used to help Auntie when we stayed with her before. We showered regularly and had a bedtime. I always slept with Mom, and Vincent started sleeping in his own bed without me. Valorie and Vance had their own beds too. I woke up every morning giving thanks that I wasn't dreaming. Our mother loved us like the moms on TV. We were normal.

Mom told us to be as helpful as we could around the house because our aunt and uncle wouldn't take any money, not even for food. My auntie said she loved Mom like a daughter. They said we were family and helping us was what family did. My aunt didn't work, and my Uncle Ted had just retired from the S&W food packing company. He'd worked there for over thirty-five years just like my grandpa Earl had at Gates rubber plant near Littleton Colorado. My uncle Ted and my grandpa Earl never missed a day of work.

Uncle Ted told us that when he first came to America, he was an immigrant, and immigrants had to prove themselves by working hard. The American Dream was what immigrants came for.

I was an immigrant too, and finding Mom was my American Dream.

Uncle Ted had a whole basement full of canned vegetables and glass jars filled with different kinds of jams and jellies all stamped with the S&W mark on them. There were shelves from the floor to the ceiling filled with string beans, corn, tomatoes, and every other fruit and vegetable you could think of. It was like a grocery store down there. I loved sorting all the cans and putting them in order by what was in them. I stacked them high, put them in alphabetical order, and faced them forward; it made it easier for my auntie to find what she needed. Doing this was another way of being helpful.

Uncle Ted said I was the most organized twelve-year-old he had ever met. I felt proud when he said that. I liked putting things in order. As long as I could remember, neatness had been important to me. Folding the napkins at Lee's Coffee Shop had been one of my favorite jobs. At St. Clara's, I'd organized the little children's clothes and put them neatly where they belonged every day. Now, I loved matching all Mom's necklaces with the correct pair of earrings. Each set had its own box with its color written on the top; this helped Mom when it was time for her to get dressed. I also lined up all of Mom's shoes in the bottom of her closet, making sure there was a matching purse on the shelf right above them. Sometimes I would stare at the organized shelves in the basement or the shoes in Mom's closet, or the neat little boxes in Mom's drawer. It made me feel happy inside when I was done organizing.

My auntie taught me how to do laundry "the right way." One afternoon, she found me on the back porch, putting clothes into her Maytag Gyrator, and she stopped me.

"You never put whites in with colored clothes, Veronica, because it will turn your whites dingy gray," she told me. When she said that, it made me think of my dishwater-blond hair.

We did the laundry together. I wanted to do the whites first, hoping to make my new white blouse look better. My first white blouse had worn out a year ago, and I'd found one almost like it the last time Bob had taken us to the Goodwill; but it wasn't really new . . . it was just new to me.

"Most important," Auntie Feling said. "Never overfill the washing machine with clothes."

In went my white blouse and my dingy white socks. Vance and Vincent's T-shirts and socks went in too, and Valorie's white bra. Mom said Val needed a new one because the one Esther had bought her was way too small. Auntie put in a few white dishtowels and, lastly, the Breeze laundry detergent. The Gyrator was ready.

After all the twisting and turning with lots of suds, it was time for the rinse. Auntie showed me how to put one cap of Mrs. Stewart's Bluing in the rinse water; this, she said, was what made everything white. I couldn't figure out how dark blue dye made white clothes whiter! I thought of the rabbit ears and how surprised I was when they made the TV work.

Once the rinsing part stopped, Auntie showed me how to slowly push the clean clothes through the wringer—that was two rolling pins put together—being careful not to get your fingers caught. The wringer made all the water come out of the clothes. Wow! My white blouse looked whiter than I'd ever seen it. The Bluing worked, just like the rabbit ears!

After all the wet clean clothes were wrung out and in the laundry basket, Auntie and I went out to the backyard, where I handed the clean clothes, one at a time, to her and she shook them out and used wooden clothes pins to hang them on the line.

Washing clothes became my second-favorite thing to do, next to organizing. When laundry needed to be done again, I decided to put a little more of Mrs. Stewart's Bluing in the rinse water to make my white blouse look brand-new. Well, that didn't work out too well; my white blouse tuned blue!

No one got mad or called me stupid. The only thing Mom said was, "More isn't always better, Veronica, remember that. It's like when you're cooking: a little salt helps food taste good but too much will ruin the pot."

I loved it when Mom didn't yell, and how she explained things to me. She taught me something new every day. I wanted to grow up to be like Mom.

(I still didn't understand how the Mrs. Stewart's Bluing made things white.)

## Chapter 35:

# OUR NEW HOME

Mom found an apartment right down the street from my aunt and uncle. It was time to have our own home. Mom didn't want to take advantage of Auntie Feling and Uncle Ted's hospitality any longer. I'd learned a lot during our stay with my aunt and uncle, but Mom was right: it was time for her to take care of us, just like she had in the Philippines.

Our new home was an upstairs two-bedroom apartment on Vendome Street. Vincent and I went with Mom to pay our first month's rent. I felt sad leaving the home we'd known for the past month but excited about having our own place. The best part was, we were still close by. I would miss the Gyrator washing machine and all the cans and jars in the basement, but I would miss Champ, Auntie Feling and Uncle Ted's little dog, the most. My auntie was happy we hadn't moved far; Mom was too.

The new apartment was a lot smaller than my aunt and uncle's house, but I didn't care, it was more beautiful than all the places we'd lived in with Bob. Fixing up the apartment with Mom was fun. We hung pictures and curtains that Mom made with the sewing machine my aunt had given her. ("It's just collecting dust," Auntie said, but I never saw any dust on it.)

Hanging things up in our new apartment reminded me of putting up the souvenirs on the coffee shop door. Mom had the bigger of the two bedrooms. There was an extra bed in her room for Vincent, and she called it a day bed, even though it was for sleeping at night. Valorie and I had our own room with twin beds, and our own closet. Mom even bought matching Beatles bedspreads for us. Vance turned the small kitchen nook into his bedroom. The man who'd rented us the apartment said the nook was where people sat for breakfast.

Mom made a navy-blue curtain for Vance's nook because it didn't have a door. It was much nicer than the gray sheet that had hung in the garage we'd last lived in with Bob.

Vance made sure his room was completely dark at night. I didn't tell Mom why he had to have his room dark. I didn't tell her about Bob leaving him next to the tree with a flashlight to teach him a lesson. Vance had made me promise never to tell. He didn't want Mom to think he was a sissy too.

Vance, Vincent, and I enrolled at Commonwealth Elementary, walking distance from our new apartment. Valorie was in the seventh grade so she went to Virgil Junior High, a little farther away. Soon after we moved, Uncle Ted drove us to May Company to get new clothes for school. Mom got rid of most of our clothes in the army duffel bag. She mended the ones she could, but the rest were either too small or not fixable.

Mom made Valorie and me dresses. She let us pick our own patterns. May Company had a whole sewing department with drawers full of patterns. Mom, Valorie, and I sat on stools at a tall table filled with thick books—*McCalls*, *Simplicity*, *Butterick*, *Vogue*. There were patterns for everything from evening gowns to nightgowns. You picked a picture of what you wanted and inside the envelope was a pattern made of paper thinner than tissue paper. Then you went to the rolls and rolls of material and got to pick whatever you wanted to make your dress out of. Doing that with Mom was more fun than anything I could think of.

I told Mom about Goodwill and said we could save money by shopping there. She liked my idea, and we went there too. Everything we did with Mom was fun, even shopping at Goodwill. Mom got things for our kitchen and clothes for the boys to play in. Valorie and I found things like jeans and sweaters—clothes we couldn't make from our patterns. Everything was turning out to be alright, just like Mom had said it would.

## Chapter 36:

# OVERQUALIFIED

Mom called a family meeting, a time when she would talk to us about family business. She told us we had to budget our money until she got a job. On four white envelopes, she wrote "Rent," "Groceries," "Utilities," and "Miscellaneous," and she kept them in a kitchen drawer. "Miscellaneous" was money for extra things. She told us that when the money for the month was gone, we'd have to make do until the beginning of the following month. If there was anything left over, we'd go to the movies or Norm's restaurant to eat.

"We have to work together," Mom said. That meant we couldn't waste anything, like food or shampoo. We turned out the lights when we left a room, and we wore socks to bed when it was cold. Doing these little things helped us save money. My lolo in the Philippines had lent Mom enough money to get by for the next couple of months.

Finding a job was Mom's main goal now. At first, she had a hard time finding a job because everywhere she applied, they told her she was *overqualified*. I asked her what that meant, and she said her master's degree in English kept her from getting a regular job. It was like she'd gone to school too much!

After being turned down a few more times, Mom decided to write on her application that she had a high school diploma. It worked! She got a job right away. This wasn't really lying, because she did have a high school diploma; she just didn't mention her bachelor's or master's degree. Mom's next goal was to be a teacher, but she needed a special certificate to work in a classroom.

When we got home from school every day, it was our job to take care of the house and get our homework done. Valorie and I cooked dinner on the three nights Mom had her night class. Mom was impressed at what a good cook Valorie was. I told Mom that Valorie could make Nail Soup. I still loved that story. I'd told it over and over to Vincent when he was little and made it different every time.

Mom made $1.25 an hour working at Bank of America as a teller. To make extra money, she fixed clothes with the sewing machine Auntie had given her and cleaned a rich person's house on Saturdays.

The best day of the week was Sunday, the Lord's Day. Mom reminded us that a person shouldn't work on this sacred day; that was the fourth Commandment. Sundays were for church and being with your loved ones. Mom lived by the Ten Commandments. I wanted to live the way God wanted me to because He'd kept his promise to me.

⁂

Mom got a raise after just a few months as a bank teller. Now she no longer had to clean the Millers' house on Saturdays. She was the new accounts assistant manager for the bank. Her job was to help people open checking and savings accounts. She even took us to the bank to show us around and introduce us to her boss, Sunny, who was the bank manager. I had never met a woman boss before.

Mom opened a savings account for me, since I had just gotten a babysitting job for a married couple on our street. I was only allowed to babysit a few hours on Friday and Saturday, while the people went to dinner or a movie. Mom said I would enjoy watching my money grow, and I did. I put half of everything I made in my savings account and the other half I gave to Mom. I made a lot of money babysitting. They paid me fifty cents an hour because they had three children and I cleaned up their house while I watched them. I told Mom I used to make ten cents for more than an hour of helping Mr. Jackson, my school janitor. I showed her my secret box where I used to keep my money. A savings account was a better place because the bank gave you interest; that's free money.

Vance and Vincent wanted a savings account too, so they decided to hunt for empty soda bottles on Saturdays. You got a penny for each bottle you turned into Reliable Market. Vance hit the jackpot, like in Las Vegas, when he found a construction site nearby. The workers threw their empty bottles everywhere. Vance and Vincent turned in fifteen to twenty bottles every time they went to Reliable Market. They never did open a savings account, though, because as soon as they got fifty cents, they spent it on candy and comic books.

Life got better and better the two years we lived in our first apartment. Then, in 1965, we moved to a three-bedroom duplex, which was more like a house and was closer to our school. Vance and I had started at Virgil Junior High just before our move. Valorie was in the ninth grade, I was in eighth, and Vance was in seventh; Vincent was in the third grade and getting tall. When we moved, he transferred to Rosemont Elementary, which was right across the street from our duplex.

Mom had gotten her teaching credential and started applying for teaching jobs, but until she got a permanent position, she substituted for teachers that were out sick or had a family emergency. She traveled every day to a different school in the LA school district. Because she couldn't take the bus to all those schools, she bought a used car from her friend Jimmy. It was a big yellow Oldsmobile with a white top and looked new, inside and out. Jimmy didn't have a wife or any children, so that's probably why his car looked perfect.

I loved Jimmy. He was funny and nice and didn't drink alcohol. Jimmy started coming every weekend to visit us, but I thought mostly Mom. On Saturdays he brought us sweet bread called *ensaïmada* from the Filipino bakery. Jimmy was Filipino and drove a shiny new red Cougar. He told me he bought a new car every five years. The Oldsmobile he'd sold Mom had been his last car.

Jimmy worked for Columbia Studios as a grip; he'd started there as an errand boy when he was a teenager. He was an immigrant, just like Uncle Ted. I asked him if he'd ever missed a day of work. He said, "No." He was just like Uncle Ted and Grandpa Earl.

On Saturday mornings, as soon as Jimmy arrived, I made him coffee to go with his *ensaïmada* and he gave me a fifty-cent piece. I told him that was too much money, but he just left it on the table and then winked at me.

I was Jimmy's favorite, and everyone knew it. Mom told him he spoiled me too much when he bought me my first pair of white go-go boots. I'd never been spoiled before and I loved it—and my boots! I wiped down my go-go boots every night and put them up on my shelf. Valorie was not allowed to even try them on.

Wherever I went with Jimmy, he would tell people I was his daughter, and then he'd wink at me. It was our special signal that we had between us. He acted like a real father should. After we were done eating our *ensaïmada* with coffee or milk, Jimmy would go downstairs and wash his and Mom's cars. He called it detailing. You couldn't find a speck of dirt when he was finished. I liked that he was so neat. Everything in his glove compartment was well organized: maps were wrapped neatly with a rubber band, sunglasses were in their case, a small notebook with a pen fit perfectly together. The trunk of his car was even neater.

Jimmy took over the job of taking us to church on Sundays, even though Mom had her own car now. I wore my go-go boots with every outfit. After church, Jimmy drove us to the Carnation Ice Cream Company on Wilshire Boulevard, where we ate lunch and then had ice cream. We did the same things every weekend: coffee, *ensaïmada*, and car detailing on Saturdays, then church and Carnation ice cream on Sundays. I looked forward to the weekends.

Once Valorie turned sixteen, she didn't like going with us as much. She wanted to be with her friends and her boyfriend. Mom let her go out on Saturdays but not Sundays; Sunday was reserved for church and the family.

On Saturday nights, Jimmy started taking Mom to dances. Sometimes they'd go to the Palladium in Hollywood or the Ambassador Hotel. Mom looked beautiful when he came to pick her up. She made most of her evening dresses and wore matching high heels and jewelry.

Jimmy loved Mom but she wouldn't marry him because of us. She told Jimmy we were her priority but maybe once we were all out of high school, she'd consider it. Jimmy made Mom laugh and always bought her beautiful gifts. My favorite gift was a mink wrap that she wore when they went dancing on Saturday nights. Jimmy was Mom's boyfriend, but I don't know if she loved him as much as he loved her.

One night, I found Mom reading a long letter from the Philippines. She said it was from a man named Mario. She told me she'd almost married him. He'd helped Mom come to America through his connections in the Philippine government. He'd even paid for Mom's flight and bought her a set of light blue Samsonite suitcases. The small one was just for makeup and had a mirror on the inside. Mom said Mario owned a shipping company and would give all of us a good life if she brought us back to the Philippines.

I asked Mom if she loved Mario, and she said, "Yes, very much." I saw tears in her eyes and told her we should go back to the Philippines and she could marry Mario and have an easier life.

Mom said it was impossible. She was writing a letter to Mario, telling him to marry someone else because Bob refused to sign a paper that would allow us to go back with her. That didn't make any sense to me since Bob had taken us out of the Philippines without Mom's signature.

Mom said it was complicated and it was best this way for her and Mario. It had been three years since she had last seen Mario and it wouldn't be fair to ask him to wait for her when she knew she'd never be able to take us 'til we were eighteen. He was younger than Mom and didn't have children. She said he loved children and she prayed he'd have his own.

At that moment, I realized what my mother had given up to rescue us. She was working hard in the United States to take care of us instead of marrying Mario, whom she loved and who loved her, and who would have given her a life of luxury with maids and everything. I started to worry that Mom might miss Mario so much, she'd want to go back to the Philippines. I wondered if we were too much trouble and cost too much money, like Bob used to say.

My eyes filled with tears. "Would you go back without us?" I asked.

Mom hugged me. "I fought too long and too hard getting all of you back. I'll never leave any of you for anything or anybody. You children are my life."

I believed her. I never doubted my mother's love again.

## Chapter 37:

# TEENAGERS

Valorie was the only one who spoke to our father anymore. Bob called her once a month at first; then it was every two months. Eventually, he stopped calling and Valorie stopped asking why. She was getting busy with her new friends at Belmont High School; I don't think she cared about hearing from Bob anymore.

It was 1966, and Valorie was sixteen and in the tenth grade. I thought of Esther when she turned sixteen, but Val was a hundred times smarter than Esther. She was a good writer and had a bigger vocabulary than any one in her class or even the school. Because of how smart she was, her journalism teacher asked her to write a monthly column for the school paper. Her column was called "What's on your mind?" She got asked about the lousy food in the cafeteria, or what to do if you were grounded, and if joining the army was a good idea. It was like a *Dear Abby* column. I don't know how

Valorie came up with the answers, but she was good at it and the column was popular.

There was a cute boy with curly brown hair and green eyes named David who was a senior and had a car. David liked Val and she liked him. No one called her Fat Val anymore; she was popular, beautiful, and smart. Valorie liked being popular and for the first time she didn't feel like an outcast. She liked the attention she was getting from boys. She wore makeup and a push-up bra. Mom let Val and me take the bus to May Company to buy bras. Mom thought it would be nice for sisters to shop together. She instructed Valorie to help me. I didn't want a bra, though, and Valorie bought the push-up one.

Belmont was in the opposite direction of Virgil Junior High, so Vance and I didn't walk to school with Valorie anymore. David picked her up in the morning and if there was time, he'd drop Vance and me off at Virgil. Both our schools were full of students from different countries: Chinese kids, black kids, and lots of Mexican kids. People in Los Angeles didn't seem to care where you came from or what you looked like—not like in Mississippi. Everyone got along with each other in school, unless they belonged to rival gangs. There were girl gangs and boy gangs.

At Virgil, most of the girls only cared about clothes, makeup, and making out with boys. If you wanted to be really popular, you could join the Syntistics, which was a girl gang at Virgil. To show how tough you were, you had to tattoo your middle finger and then cover it with a ring so your parents wouldn't see it. A friend in typing class joined and wanted me to join too. I knew Mom wouldn't approve of me tattooing my finger, so I told a little lie: "My mother will throw me out of the house if she finds out and I don't have a father, so I won't have a place to live!" That seemed to work. I was relieved, especially after I found out that not only did you have to have a tattoo, you also had to get beat up by the other girls to make it in.

Making out with lots of boys was another way to be popular, but I wasn't interested in doing that either. Valorie told me she made out with David all the time in his car. She also said she had sex with him in his car. After what had happened in Texas, I was shocked when she said that. How could she let that happen? I told her Mom wouldn't approve but Valorie just said, "What she doesn't know won't hurt her." It hurt me when she said that because it was disrespectful to our mother, and because I felt that her having sex with David was disrespectful to herself.

Being fifteen and in the ninth grade was a big deal at my school; we were practically in high school. I didn't feel like a scared, insecure little girl anymore. I had stopped wondering what people thought of me every time they glanced my way. I reminded myself daily that I was normal—had a normal life. People didn't make fun of normal people. I was able to hold my head up without thinking about it. Making my mother proud and getting good grades was what I strived for, and I was doing both. I had lots of friends even though I didn't make out with boys and hadn't joined a gang. I wore nice clothes and was smart. I felt on top of the world.

---

One hot summer's day in 1967, I was standing in line at a 7-Eleven buying an RC Cola after school. I was nervous because I was graduating and going to be crowned "Most Likely to Succeed" at the 7-10 dance that night. Virgil Junior High had a dance on the last Friday of every month called the 7-10 Dance, and tonight was going to be my last one; the whole school was going to be there.

As I stood in the slow-moving line at the 7-Eleven, all I could think about was what to wear that night. I decided on the baby blue mini-dress I'd made in my home economics class; I'd gotten an A+ on it. The dress fit me snugly on top with an empire waist, then flared out at the bottom. The dress code at my school required that the length of your dress not be shorter than the tip of your finger when your arm was at your side. I cheated a little by bending my elbow when being measured so my dress would be an inch shorter.

Mom had been teaching me how to sew these past two years, and I had gotten pretty good with the sewing machine. Today, as I stood in line, I was wearing the white skirt I had made as my final project for the year. My teacher had complimented me on how well done it was. No more safety pins for me. I had even put in the zipper without help. As I stood in line, I was feeling particularly pretty, which made me stand taller.

While standing there, I started thinking about a cute guy named Allen. I was hoping he'd talk to me or ask me to dance that night. As I placed the ice-cold RC next to my cheek, two older men standing behind me started whispering and laughing to each other. I didn't pay any attention until one of them moved in so close he was almost touching me, then said in a low voice, "I'd like to bend you over and lift that skirt, little girl."

I flashed back to the time Bob said, "You're not very pretty, Veronica, so if you want a man, just lift that dress." I put the RC down right where I stood and ran out of the store. I'd lost my self-worth in those four years with Bob, and just when I thought I was getting some of it back I felt punched in the stomach and wanted to scream.

Being away from my father didn't mean being away from people like him; they just came in different packages. Mom couldn't protect me as I got older. I had to learn how to fight my own battles. Who were the good guys and who were the bad ones? Good guys didn't always wear white; they came in all colors, shapes, and ages. I wanted to feel stronger, not just smarter. How would I keep from running out of the next 7-Eleven? There had to be away to defend myself besides hitting someone, even though I did want to kick that guy in his private parts.

---

One day, after a year of not hearing from our father, Valorie received a letter from Bob telling her that he'd moved to San Francisco and married Rita. Rita with the Mercedes!? What little I knew about Bob came from Valorie. I wasn't curious and never asked, but she felt it was important to let me know what he was up to.

Valorie started writing letters back to Bob, asking if she could visit him in San Francisco. She said there were popular rock and roll bands she wanted to see that played at the Fillmore.

In 1967, when Valorie was seventeen, she went to spend half of her summer with our father. Mom told her to call every day, but she didn't. When she did call, she told me she'd seen Janis Joplin and Jefferson Airplane. I didn't care; my friends and I were more into Motown. But The Beatles were still my favorite.

When Valorie got back from San Francisco that summer, she was different. She looked different and dressed different. She considered herself a hippie and told me she'd smoked *grass* with our father, and he'd let her do whatever she wanted.

It's hard to explain how I felt being away from Bob. It had been four years since we'd lived with him; the same amount of time we had spent with him. The four years with our father had seemed like an eternity, but with Mom, the time flew by. My life was so normal that I'd almost forgotten I had a father, and I didn't want to be reminded by Valorie. Once I heard a girl say, "Out of sight, out of mind," when she was talking about her ex-boyfriend. That described exactly how I felt about Bob.

Valorie and I didn't agree on anything regarding Bob, music, drugs, or boys, which caused us to drift apart. She called me a "mama's girl," and said that I was a "downer."

Being called a mama's girl didn't bother me one bit because it was true. Being called a downer, which was a person who was no fun, didn't bother me either.

Valorie hated that I called our father Bob; she said it was impertinent. I had to look that word up. How was it that we saw Bob so differently? He and Mom were like day and night.

After the summer with Bob, Valorie started going out most weekends and stopped going to church with us. Mom worried about my sister, but she let her go because she didn't know what else to do; she just had to trust her and trust that God would watch over her. I hated seeing Mom upset and blamed Valorie for making her sad. Mom was our angel, our savior; how could Valorie not listen to her? The idea of leaving Mom or giving her anything to worry about never even entered my mind.

Vance was friends with a couple of boys on our block who were fourteen too. They rode bikes together and hung out at each other's houses. Vance's best friend, Henry had two older brothers who belonged to a club called Clanton or 14th St. Vance looked up to them and wanted to be in their club.

Vance said the guys in the club took care of each other. No one messed with any of them because they'd fight anyone who tried. It was like having twenty brothers protecting you.

Vance liked being accepted by his newfound friends and started hanging out with them more than with Vincent and me. When he turned sixteen, he did become a member. It turned out to be a gang, not a social club.

Mom was busy teaching in the day and going to school at night again. This time, she went every night to get her Special Education Credential. This new credential would allow her to teach at Widney High, a special education high school. She would make more money and be teaching handicapped students. Mom loved teaching, but teaching students who needed special help was what she really wanted to do.

As long as we got our homework and chores done, Mom let us go out with our friends. She said we were old enough to take care of ourselves but told us to always leave a note as to where we were. Vance always left the same note—that he was with Henry. I never had to leave a note because I'd rather be home waiting for Mom. Valorie was everywhere and anywhere. Vincent was eleven and hung out with me in the house most the time. He did have a best friend, though, a girl named Linley. Sometimes they'd stay out 'til after dark, and I'd have to look for him before Mom got home. Vincent and Linley were inseparable. They were always at our house or her house. They played board games together or just talked on the porch. She was the only one in the neighborhood that was Vincent's age. Linley had red hair and greenish eyes, and Vincent had a crush on her.

On school nights we watched TV together after our homework was done. My favorite show was *Petticoat Junction*. Vance and Vincent like *Bonanza*, and Mom's favorite was *The*

*Lawrence Welk Show.* Valorie usually went to her room to read or write in her diary—probably about her latest boyfriend. Saturdays were usually just Mom, Jimmy, Vincent, and me now. Vance and Valorie were usually with their friends. Jimmy still detailed both his and Mom's cars, and we still went to Carnation's Ice Cream after church on Sundays.

Sundays were supposed to be family days but most the time Valorie wasn't home for them, and she never went to church. She told me she was an atheist. I asked her what that meant, and she said, "Look it up dummy!"

I hated Valorie at that moment. I did look it up and swore to myself that I'd never tell Mom what Valorie had said, because I knew that her being an atheist would make Mom cry.

Becoming teenagers seemed to pull us apart. The day Valorie graduated from Belmont, she moved out with her boyfriend, Richard. She was eighteen, and there was nothing Mom could say to convince her not to. Vance was sixteen then and considered his friends in Clanton his brothers.

When he turned seventeen, Vance got arrested for fighting a rival gang. Mom had to pick him up from the police station; her being a teacher helped get him out. It was the first time he'd been in trouble with the police, so Mom gave him a choice: juvenile hall or joining the army. Vance picked the army; he was finally going to be a real live G. I. Joe. When he turned seventeen, Mom signed a paper and he was off to Fort Ord.

At eighteen, I was still a mama's girl. I liked boys, one in particular, but never thought of doing anything that Mom wouldn't approve of. When my boyfriend started pressuring me to have sex, we broke up. I was the only one of my friends that hadn't *done it* yet. By the time I was a senior, I'd made up a story about a college boy I was dating off and on. When my close friends asked if we were having sex, I'd say, "What do you think?" and then drop the subject. It wasn't a lie; I just let them draw their own conclusion. Growing up in the sixties, being eighteen and not participating in *free love* or doing LSD made me a downer; I wasn't invited to very many cool parties.

I never told anyone about what had happened to Valorie in Texas. A drunk soldier had forced her to have sex with him, and he'd hurt her. Having an alcoholic father made me never want to do drugs, and my time at St. Clara's had made the thought of taking my clothes off horrifying to me. I hadn't gotten over the indecency of the naked body. I'd worn my underwear in the shower 'til I was fourteen; only then did it finally dawn on me that I was alone and no one was looking. I couldn't even look at myself naked in the mirror; it seemed repulsive.

By the time I was a senior, Valorie and Vance were Mom's greatest worry. Valorie was doing hard drugs, and Vance had gotten beaten up in boot camp and ended up in the hospital.

Mom lit a candle at her makeshift altar before going to bed every night. I promised myself I wasn't going to add to her worry. I promised God I'd never upset my mother.

I talked to Mom about Vincent going to King Jr. High. I didn't want Vincent at Virgil or Belmont because I could see the direction Vance was going in, and Vincent looked up to Vance. Vincent had long hair and he hung out with kids that went to King, which was a mostly white school near Hollywood. Vincent didn't want to go to Virgil. "It's a Cholo school," he said, and he told me he was afraid of getting picked on because of his long hair. Cholos didn't like Longhairs.

When Vincent turned thirteen, he moved in with his best friend's family who lived near King Junior High. Vincent had to have an address in the district, so Carl's parents let the boys live in their basement. I helped Vincent convince Mom to let him live with Carl's family. She finally agreed because she could see how badly he wanted to go to King.

Vincent ended up never living with us again after that. He got a part-time job to pay for food and lived with Carl's family for the next two years.

Valorie, Vance, and Vincent loved Mom and visited her often, but from 1969 to 1972, my mother found it difficult to communicate with them. I don't think Mom was prepared for how different American culture was from Philippines culture; in her family, Lolo's word was law, with no negotiating or saying, "I don't want to."

In 1969, Mom was hired full-time at Widney High School. Her students loved her and were more grateful than the kids she'd taught in public schools. Mom had found her perfect job. She enjoyed teaching every day. The principal, Mr. Small, told Mom she had a gift for teaching children with mental and physical disabilities. From the janitor to the principal to every student at the school, everyone at Widney loved my mother. It was easy to love Mom; she was a living saint.

## Chapter 38:

# FREE AT LAST

Mom was proud of me when I received my scholarship to UCLA in 1970. Her goal was for all of us to go to college. Because I realized I'd be the only one, it became my goal too. My counselor had told me about a scholarship being offered through a law called *affirmative action*. The law required schools to diversify their student body by accepting kids of other cultures.

If it wasn't for affirmative action, I wouldn't have been able to attend a university; Mom couldn't afford it. What qualified me was my GPA, plus the fact that I was Filipino, female, and had a financial need. After a short interview, I was in.

My full scholarship stipulated that I had to live in the dorms on campus. As much as I wanted to go to college, the thought of leaving home caused my old insecurities to raise their ugly heads. At orientation, the girls in my dorm, Hedrick Hall, were mostly white, drove nice cars, and had money. I had frequent anxiety attacks being separated from my mother, even at nineteen. Living in the dorm was mandatory to keep my scholarship, though, so I had to stay.

Jimmy didn't want me to take the bus home on Fridays, so he surprised me with a used Chevy II. He was proud of me too. Mom and Jimmy were still going out, but I think he wanted more. Mom held firm to making sure her children were grown and done with school before she'd consider anything more than good friends.

There was another lady named Josie that liked Jimmy a lot, and I saw him flirting with her at a party once. I told Mom but she said, "If he cares for me, he'll wait." Mom was strong, independent, a warrior.

I would drive my Chevy II home in the middle of the week when the dorm got to be too overwhelming. I'd show up at Mom's door and sleep in her bed, and then I'd get up at the crack of dawn to make it back to the dorms and then my classes. My roommate, Julie, was half Japanese and half white. We chose each other during orientation because we were both Amerasian. Julie had a white boyfriend, Bruce, who spent the night all the time. When they made too much noise, I'd grab my blanket and pillow and sleep in the dorm lounge.

One night, Bruce brought his older brother, Mike, with him. He was visiting from Louisiana, where he played basketball. Mike was cute and seemed nice. After hanging out and talking in our dorm room for a while, he invited all of us to walk down to Westwood to get some food.

Westwood was a lot of fun because it was where all the UCLA students hung out. There was always something going on; if not a protest, then music being played in the street.

When we got back to the dorm, Mike informed me that he was spending the night. Why couldn't I just say "no?" I was really uncomfortable, but he insisted and said, "It's settled." Julie and Bruce left, and I felt petrified. I wasn't as strong as my mother. She would have thrown him out but that wasn't what I did. I felt overpowered by men, and in situations like this one, I lost my voice.

I later found out that Julie had told Bruce I was a virgin and he'd told his brother. They'd made a bet at my expense.

Mike won.

I hated myself for the rest of the year. Julie tried to comfort me by saying, "It's not a big deal Veronica, you had to do it sometime!" I drove home almost every night for the next couple of months. I didn't tell anyone what had happened. I never heard from Mike again.

UCLA was painful. I felt alone on the huge campus, missed my family, and was once again in a school where I felt the white kids looked down on me and the boys just wanted me to lift my skirt. The four forever years with my father continued to interfere with my life. But I had to find a way to survive UCLA. I couldn't quit. I wasn't going to disappoint my mother. I wanted to be the warrior woman Mom was when she went to the University of Boulder. That school had also been a predominantly white school and people had made fun of her, but she'd held her head up and hadn't let anyone stop her from reaching her goal.

I was lonely at UCLA, even though there were plenty of students around me at Hedrick Hall. I ate alone in the cafeteria, pretending to be reading. I didn't go to parties, date, or join any clubs on campus. Sororities and football games didn't interest me at all.

Then I started listening to speakers on campus—people like Jane Fonda and Cesar Chavez. They spoke against social injustice, unfair labor laws, and the Vietnam War, and talked about women's rights. In those mesmerizing moments, I discovered activism. Talk about a silver lining!

Activism brought out the part of me that was my mother. The protests were empowering and led me to my most significant college experiences. I was able to express what I thought and how I felt about what was going on around me. I was hungry to learn as much as I could. I met interesting people who I felt comfortable talking to. I made friends and together, we protested the Vietnam War, attended rallies, listened to Angela Davis, and marched with Cesar Chavez in support of the farm workers. These were amazing, powerful, brave people who were making a difference and changing lives—other people's lives, and mine. They were warriors, not victims.

I learned what it meant to be a feminist while at UCLA and, to my surprise, discovered women had rights! No meant no. Bob was all wrong about me, about women. I had a voice, and I was going to make myself heard.

Being active in social movements was what got me through UCLA. Marching in anti-war rallies showed me that you could make a difference in the things you believed in. My strength erupted deep within me, like a volcano. I felt like a phoenix rising from the ashes.

I finally found what truly set me free: me.

# EPILOGUE

*"Success is not final; failure is not fatal; it is the courage to continue that counts."*

—Winston S. Churchill

After UCLA, I went on to medical school and earned a Doctor of Chiropractic degree. I married several times but have only one child, Francis, who was born in 1986. He is the love of my life.

I practiced my profession for thirty-five years in Santa Monica and Palm Springs. I loved being a doctor as much as Mom loved teaching. She always told me to follow my passion and I wouldn't go wrong. She was right. I retired on Maui in 2017 and brought my beautiful mother with me. Mom never married, and Jimmy married Josie. Jimmy and I continued to be in each other's lives until he died in 2010. He died telling me he still loved my mother.

Mom died peacefully on March 15, 2019, along with a part of me. She was ninety-five.

I had finally become the woman she was. I made her proud, and she showed me her love every day. Her ashes are buried on my property, on the hill by the black bamboo.

We will continue to be together in life and in death. She was what I prayed for.

Mom and I, Maui, 2018

Mom on her 95th birthday

# POST-SCRIPT

## *Valorie*

Valorie was brilliant and could have done anything in life. She was a writer, a poet, and a logophile who spoke eloquently. You never would have guessed that a high school education was the sum total of her academic foundation. It was amazing how many books she read as a child. We loved it when the Library on Wheels came around when we lived in Mississippi. For every book I checked out, Val checked out five or six. The first few years after Bob, she buried herself in science fiction novels and padlocked diaries.

My big sister fought an ongoing battle with depression. When we were young, she used reading to escape her pain. No matter how normal life appeared on the outside as we grew older, the Bob years haunted her. When she was eleven, Valorie was sexually assaulted by a soldier from Fort Hood. There was a trial and he was found guilty, but Bob should have been found guilty as well for putting Valorie in the perfect setting to be raped: alone on a farm in the middle of nowhere with a twenty-eight-year-old drunken soldier as our babysitter. We were all there that night and couldn't help her; it was our shared nightmare.

Valorie was the smartest person I knew growing up. She seemed to know the answers to all our questions. When I found out she wasn't interested in going to college, I was sad. Drugs, both prescription and street, had become her ticket out of the mental anguish that held her prisoner. She lived with a boyfriend whose drug of choice was heroin. Together, they'd transport themselves to a place where life was tolerable.

Valorie married four times, had two sons, and two granddaughters that she adored.

Mom didn't understand what Valorie was going through and had no idea how deep her drug addiction was. Val never told Mom her secrets; none of us did.

I tried talking to Valorie over the years, but she developed a defiant streak that threw up a wall between us; I was just the spoiled little sister who had it all. I never shared my hidden pain with her because she had enough of her own, but now I see that sharing was exactly what we both needed.

Coming from another culture, Mom struggled with what to do for her eldest daughter, and in the end, she found it easier to accept whatever it was that Valorie wanted to do; nothing was going to stop her anyway.

For a long time, I thought Mom loved Valorie more than me because she got permission without an argument whenever she wanted to do anything. I, on the other hand, worked hard to make Mom proud. I was the good child, the child who did everything right, the child who never worried her, yet Mom was much stricter with me. I was jealous of

Mom's long talks with Valorie and how it was always Valorie she took places.

When I was in my early thirties, I mentioned to Mom how jealous I'd been, as a teenager, at the amount of love Valorie received over me.

Mom stopped what she was doing and looked at me with surprise. "Veronica," she said, "You are my pride and joy. My attention to your sister was because she needed me more than you did. I've never had to worry about you; you were my perfect child. Your sister needed all the help I could give her. I don't love any of you more than the other." Mom hugged me for several minutes before saying, "I'm so grateful for you, Veronica."

I wished I had asked Mom earlier; I could have saved myself years of thinking I wasn't doing enough.

The sexual abuse Valorie suffered was probably the main reason she did drugs, but I think the other reason was her inability to get the love and attention from our father that she desperately wanted. Valorie would do anything for our father, including doing drugs with him—anything to bring him closer to her.

We never talked about that darkest of nights in Florence, Texas; as children, we didn't have the words. As the years passed, we kept those memories buried to save us from reliving the pain of helplessness. I never told Valorie about the ongoing abuse I faced from our father when he was drunk, and Vance didn't talk about what he'd suffered at St. Clara's when he was only seven. By the time we were adults, our secrets had been driven deep within by drugs, alcohol, and obsessions that left no room for healthy discussions.

On Thanksgiving night, 2000, Valorie made her famed Thanksgiving dinner for the family. After a fabulous meal, we packed up and promised to get together more often. It had been a long time since the whole family had been in the same room, and it felt good. There were hugs and kisses, as we found it hard to say good-bye.

Valorie left Mom's house exhausted, thankful her husband was driving. When she got home, she took a Vicodin for her fibromyalgia and a Xanax for her anxiety and washed both down with a little red wine. She always said, "Wine to un-wine." After getting into bed with her two precious teacup poodles, she took an Ambien for her insomnia and had a little more wine. As she lay in bed watching the eleven o'clock news, still unable to fall asleep, she lit a cigarette to go with the last sip of her red wine. Valorie fell asleep with the lit cigarette still burning in her hand.

My sister died that night at forty-nine years old when her house was engulfed in flames, claiming her and her precious poodles. The fire captain found her in the master bath, curled up behind the toilet, barely alive. He said she'd tried to get out through the bathroom window, but it was protected by permanent security bars. I was devastated when the fire captain told me she probably woke up with flames covering her bed and, in her confusion, panic, and medication, ran into her bathroom, trapping herself. I hated thinking about what her last moments must have been like. It wasn't supposed to end like that. Her husband, who slept in a separate room, was seriously injured trying to save her.

Valorie accomplished many things in the last ten years of her life. She stopped doing street drugs and got involved in local government. She founded Chrysalis, a non-profit organization in Huntington Park, California, which assisted gang members and parolees in getting back on their feet after being released from prison. She helped their families with finding childcare, filling out applications, and dressing for job interviews. She also published two books, one a collection of short stories based on Filipino folklore and one a book of poems. Her most passionate project was fighting to gain US citizenship for the illegitimate children left behind in Philippines by American soldiers. I knew nothing about her altruistic accomplishments until after her death. I was too busy obsessing about my own success.

At her funeral, it was standing room only in the large Catholic church. I was shocked by how many young people came with their families. The crowd flowed out to the street, with everyone lining up to speak about their friend Valorie. They shared stories of how they were saved by her kindness, caring, and willingness to fight for them. I had no idea before that day how many lives she'd touched, and I was so proud. She finally found a way to heal herself by giving to others, and her goodness will impact generations to come. Valorie left this world a better place.

With all the pain my sister endured while we were living with Bob, she continued to love him, never blaming our father for what happened to us. She always said, "He had his reasons for doing what he did. He tried his best." I never understood how she came to that conclusion when my experience was so different.

Valorie Elisa was beautiful, brilliant, and loved by many but was unable to acknowledge her tremendous worth. Just when she was beginning to see what she was capable of, her prescription drug addiction snatched it away. I miss her beyond words.

Valorie, 1950-2000

## Vance

Then there was Vance, a sensitive little boy. It was difficult for him to understand why we left in 1959 and why we couldn't go home. He was lost and never found his footing during those four forever years. Vance spent those years searching for the security he desperately needed in order to survive but was unsuccessful; self-preservation drove him inward, and later to drugs and alcohol.

One night, Vance stopped by my house to drop off a birthday present for my son, Francis. We ended up drinking wine and talking late into the night. For the first time, he shared specific memories with me about our time with Bob. Vance was young, and his memories were sketchy, but he did talk about St. Clara's. I'd always had a gut feeling something evil had happened to him there, but we'd never talked about our darkest secrets.

After his third or fourth glass of wine, Vance started to cry. I held him and asked him what was wrong. It was then that he told me about the rape—how the sixteen- and seventeen-year-old boys held him face down, and he couldn't defend himself or tell anyone for fear of getting more of the same. We cried in each other's arms. I didn't ask questions; I just held him tight.

Vance always had well-paid jobs because he was a quick learner and dependable. He managed to keep his drinking hidden from his employers but let his guard down when he got home. His drinking finally drove his wife and children to leave him. Their separation trigged a visceral pain so great he turned to street drugs. Vance ultimately lost his job and apartment, which left him living in his car. I wasn't aware of his crack addiction or his homelessness; I was too busy being the successful doctor.

I received a phone call late one night from a hospital in the valley asking if I knew a Vance Slaughter.

"Yes," I said in a panic, "I'm his sister. What's wrong?"

The doctor reassured me that he was alive. I took a deep breath. He said someone had reported a man living in an abandoned car with a cat. I couldn't believe what I was hearing.

I learned that the police had found Vance unconscious and emaciated. My business card was all they'd found in his pocket.

I rushed to the hospital and found Vance hooked up to an IV in his room, awake but agitated. The first thing he asked was, "Where is my cat? Don't let anything happen to my cat! Please, Veronica, take care of him for me!"

I had a flashback to Fleas; how Vance had loved him, and how grief-stricken he'd been when Fleas disappeared. I promised Vance I'd take care of his cat, and he calmed down instantly.

Tearfully I asked, "Why didn't you tell me? Why didn't you come to me? How did this happen?"

"I knew how busy you were," Vance said. "I didn't want to bother you."

*God*, I thought, *how did it come to this? How did I not know that my sweet little brother was alone, drug addicted, and homeless? What happened to our forever bond?* He was living my worst nightmare, the reason I worked nonstop—and here it was, facing me through my brother.

I checked Vance out of the hospital the next day, and he came to live with me in Santa Monica. He enrolled in a medical billing course and went to AA meetings every day. Francis loved his Uncle Vance, and we became a family for the next year. When he finished school, Vance got a job at Blue Cross and began turning his life around. He loved his new job and quickly advanced in the company, got an apartment, and married for the second time.

A few years later, however, he relapsed, and his second wife filed for legal separation. Vance continued to work hard and drink at night, vowing not to end up homeless ever again. I lectured him every chance I got but eventually, I gave up. I had no control; it was up to Vance. To my surprise, his drinking didn't interfere with work and he continued to do well.

I moved to a place in the desert near Palm Springs, California, in 2005. I opened a second office and bought two condos next to one another, one for me and one to rent. Vance came out often to spend weekends with me after Francis left for Sonoma State in Northern California. One weekend, he asked if he could move into my rental. He said he was on workers' comp due to an injury called ulna entrapment, caused by repetitive use of a computer. He developed an addiction to Oxycontin after elbow surgery and needed my help.

I was furious about this new addiction and made multiple conditions he would have to abide by in order for me to agree. I don't know why I was so hard on him; I wish now that I could take back my painful words. I demanded that he go to AA meetings and not embarrass me in front of friends and neighbors. I treated him like a failure. I, of all people, should have known how it feels to be put down, but I was tired of the relapses and wanted him to "snap out of it." I refused to acknowledge his alcoholism as a disease requiring ongoing treatment. I failed to appreciate that he was doing exactly what I asked by coming to me for help. He begged my forgiveness, apologized, and agreed to my demands and more. I made everything about me when he was the one suffering.

Vance was scheduled to move into my rental May 1, 2012, right after Easter. He packed and carefully marked each box—"Veronica's house kitchen," "Veronica's house bedroom." Each box had my name and his on it. He was so excited, and left out only one plate, one glass, and a change of clothes. He wanted to be ready in case my present renters moved early.

A week before Vance was scheduled to move in, we had Easter dinner at Vincent's house in Norco. I called Vance and asked him to pick up Mom in Santa Monica and to be on time for dinner! We were well into our meal when Mom and Vance drove up, two hours late. I was fuming, assuming it had to do with his drinking. I opened the door and immediately laid into him about being unreliable. I told him I was having second thoughts about him moving in next to me because I couldn't count on him.

When I was done berating him, I noticed he was shaking. Again, I didn't give him the benefit of the doubt; I assumed the worst, thought he was probably on drugs.

When I finally shut up and let Vance explain, he told me he'd picked up Mom early but had gotten lost on a freeway he knew well, and Mom had to direct him. He said he was scared, felt shaky, and was feeling confused.

I understood right then how ill he was.

Vance died of liver cancer nine days later. He was fifty-eight.

I spent those nine days by his side, trying desperately to make up for my condescending attitude a few days earlier and praying for a miracle, I told him how sorry I was and begged for his forgiveness.

"I love you more than all the stars in the sky, Veronica," he told me. "There is nothing to forgive." That was my sweet Vance: kind, shy, forgiving.

The night before he died, I held him in bed like a mother holds her sick child. I was singing to him quietly when he whispered, "Am I going to die, Veronica?"

"Yes, my love," I said, "but I'm right here and I'm not letting you go."

We fell asleep wrapped tightly in each other's arms.

After Vance's passing, I was cleaning out his apartment when I found a card on top of one of the many boxes he'd packed in his eagerness to move in next to me. A note at the bottom of a thank-you card read, "My life wouldn't be worth living if it wasn't for you, Veronica, thank you for giving me another chance. I won't let you down."

I held the card to my chest and sank into a profound sadness.

Vance was a wonderful, sensitive, kind, loving person. He was soft-spoken and had a special place in his heart for all animals. He worked hard, which elevated him at every job he ever had. His pride and joy were his daughters and their children, who loved him unconditionally. Vance had been struggling with sobriety since he was fourteen and felt his last hope was living close to me. He trusted me with the privilege of saving his life, but I was too late.

Vance Slaughter, 1953-2012

## *Vincent*

My youngest sibling, Vincent, whom I've always considered my first child, was the main reason I made it through the dark years with Bob. He was my baby; we were inseparable. I became his mother when I was only eight years old because of a promise I'd made to our mother. With no mothering experience, I did my best to shield him from physical and emotional harm. We loved each other fully and totally. He was the love of my life, and I, his.

Vincent morphed from a chubby little three-year-old to a tall, dark, and handsome man who charmed every woman he met. His first conquest came at thirteen with our nineteen-year-old neighbor. When he was fourteen, he lived part time with his eighth-grade Spanish teacher for nine months.

When Vincent finished the tenth grade, he left school. He had severe dyslexia that had gone undiagnosed when he was young, and it made him feel that he couldn't compete in school. He survived high school on his good looks and charm 'til he just couldn't fool his teachers anymore. He wasn't diagnosed until he reached his mid-twenties.

The one class Vincent always excelled in was workshop. He learned he was good at building things with his hands. When an opportunity came up to help build a house in Colorado with a contracting friend of his when he was seventeen, he moved there. He went on to be a successful contractor in his own right.

As charming and flirtatious as Vincent was, his fear of abandonment kept him from true love. He wasn't willing to take the chance of having a woman leave him, so friends with benefits was his golden rule. He was always honest with the women in his life about not wanting long-term commitment, however. Vincent was the only man I ever knew who kept all his ex-lovers as friends.

Vincent started his own business on Maui called Hill Top Homes. He built dream homes for his clients while living his dream in Haiku, his paradise and sanctuary.

When he was around forty, he met a beautiful young woman twenty years his junior. They married and raised three incredible children. His children were what he had searched for his whole life: someone to love and forever be his. He had it all: a successful business, a wife who loved him, children to call his own, and five lush acres filled with dogs, horses, goats, and chickens.

On November 15, 2007, I ignored multiple cell phone calls because I was busy. When I finally checked my messages, they were from Vincent's wife, crying that Vincent had fallen and was in the hospital. I hurried home, not knowing how serious his injuries were. When I finally got hold of the hospital, they told me he was in a coma. I was on the next flight to Maui.

Vincent fell from the lanai of one of the condominiums he was building in Kihei. He was managing a large project with a fast-approaching deadline. He may have been the boss, but he was a builder first, and getting the project done was his priority, so instead of sitting in his office, he joined his crew. He wasn't too proud to get his hands dirty, which was one of many reasons why everyone who worked for him loved him.

When Vincent finally regained consciousness a week later, he was a quadriplegic. When I explained to him what had happened, tears ran down his face and he begged me to take him anywhere euthanasia was legal. I promised him I would if he swore to hang on for a year to see how much movement he could regain. He reluctantly agreed, fighting like the warriors from whom we are descended.

After an extended period in the hospital on Oahu, Vincent was medevac'd to California for further specialized care. The good news was, he lived. The bad news, he was paralyzed from the neck down.

My baby boy struggled for almost six years, hoping for a scientific development that would allow him to move, even if just one finger to type, push a button for help, or run a wheelchair. He had no choice but to surrender to total dependency on caregivers. He could no longer brush his own teeth, feed himself, or move from room to room without a caregiver by his side.

Riding his horses or his Harley Davidson would now happen only in his dreams. He was not—could not have been—prepared for this reality. No longer was he the strong, protective father to his children. They were on their own, abandoned like he had been; it was his worst nightmare come true.

In the end, fighting to stay alive proved to be too much for his broken body.

Vincent passed away on September 13, 2013, at fifty-seven years old. I never left his side the last few months of his life, which were the happiest and saddest days of my life.

Before he took his last breath, he asked me, "Can't you come with me, Veronica? I'm so afraid."

"I'm here and will never let you go," I told him. "I promise to join you, Valorie, and Vance shortly, but for now, my darling, you are going to be free."

Life had come full circle for Vincent and me. We held hands when we were taken from our mother; now I fought letting go as he was taken from me.

When his heart stopped, my heart broke.

They're all gone too soon.

Vincent Slaughter, 1956-2013

## ABOUT THE AUTHOR

Dr. Veronica Slaughter was born in 1951 on the island of Samar, in the Philippines. In 1959, she was abducted along with her three siblings and brought to the United States where they vanished into darkness. Despite her painful childhood, she went on to become a Doctor of Chiropractic in Southern California and practiced from 1982 to 2018. Now retired, Dr. Slaughter lives on the beautiful island of Maui. She continues to speak on the power of love and small acts of kindness toward your fellow human being; love conquers all. She has one son who lives in Northern California, and is the love of her life.

*Author photo © Dominique Pandolfi*

## SELECTED TITLES FROM SHE WRITES PRESS

She Writes Press is an independent publishing company founded to serve women writers everywhere. Visit us at www.shewritespress.com.

***I'm the One Who Got Away: A Memoir*** by Andrea Jarrell. $16.95, 978-1-63152-260-4. When Andrea Jarrell was a girl, her mother often told her of their escape from Jarrell's dangerous, cunning father as if it was a bedtime story. Here, Jarrell reveals the complicated legacy she inherited from her mother—and shares a life-affirming story of having the courage to become both safe enough and vulnerable enough to love and be loved.

***Pieces of Me: Rescuing My Kidnapped Daughters*** by Lizbeth Meredith. 978-1-63152-834-7. When her daughters are kidnapped and taken to Greece by their non-custodial father, single mom Lizbeth Meredith vows to bring them home—and give them a better childhood than her own.

***The Coconut Latitudes: Secrets, Storms, and Survival in the Caribbean*** by Rita Gardner. $16.95, 978-1-63152-901-6. A haunting, lyrical memoir about a dysfunctional family's experiences in a reality far from the envisioned Eden—and the terrible cost of keeping secrets.

***Secrets in Big Sky Country: A Memoir*** by Mandy Smith. $16.95, 978-1-63152-814-9. A bold and unvarnished memoir about the shattering consequences of familial sexual abuse—and the strength it takes to overcome them.

***Fourteen: A Daughter's Memoir of Adventure, Sailing, and Survival*** by Leslie Johansen Nack. $16.95, 978-1-63152-941-2. A coming-of-age adventure story about a young girl who comes into her own power, fights back against abuse, becomes an accomplished sailor, and falls in love with the ocean and the natural world.

***Implosion: Memoir of an Architect's Daughter*** by Elizabeth W. Garber. $16.95, 978-1-63152-351-9. When Elizabeth Garber, her architect father, and the rest of their family move into Woodie's modern masterpiece, a glass house, in 1966, they have no idea that over the next few years their family's life will be shattered—both by Woodie's madness and the turbulent 1970s.

www.ingramcontent.com/pod-product-compliance
Lightning Source LLC
Chambersburg PA
CBHW021502170125
20462CB00004B/173

* 9 7 8 1 6 3 1 5 2 7 2 5 8 *